Glimmerings I

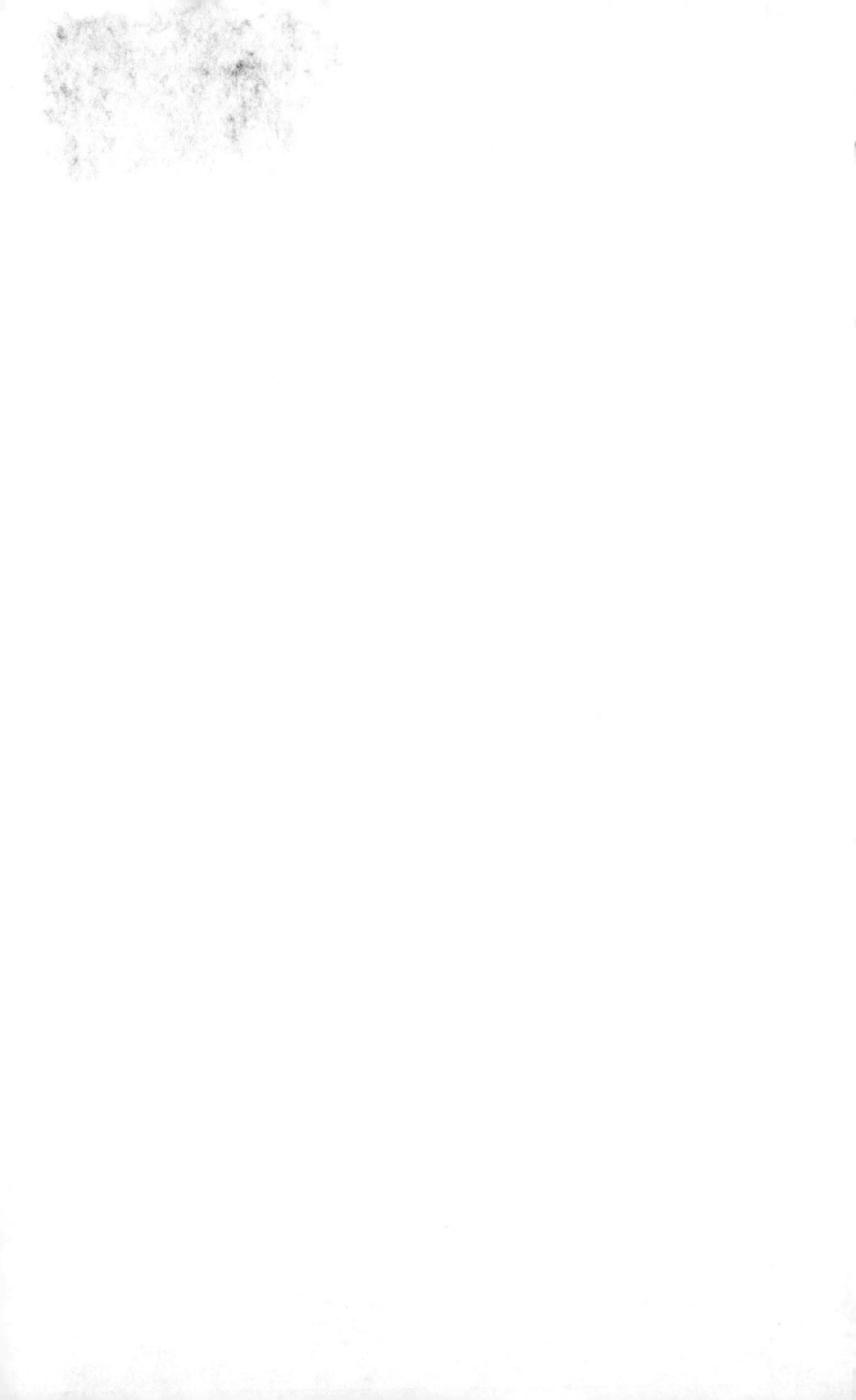

Glimmerings
I

1001 Thoughts, Ideas,
Observations, Musings
Reflections, and Comments
On Whatever Comes to Mind

Robert A. Harris

.:Virtual**Salt**
Publishing
Tustin

Glimmerings I
1001 Thoughts, Ideas, Observations, Musings, Reflections, and
Comments On Whatever Comes to Mind

ISBN 978-1-941233-08-5

VirtualSalt® Publishing
Tustin, California

www.virtualsalt.com

In the mass of materials which ingenious absurdity has thrown together, genuine wit and useful knowledge may be sometimes found.
    – Samuel Johnson, Life of Cowley

Some excellent sayings are found in very silly books, and some silly thoughts appear in books of value.
    – Isaac Watts, Logick

That book should be esteemed well written which has much more of good sense in it than it has of impertinence.
    – Isaac Watts, Logick

Why are you always telling me obvious things?
    – Former girlfriend

Philosophy is a modest profession, all simplicity and plain dealing. Never try to seduce me into solemn pretentiousness.
    – Marcus Aurelius, Meditations

Introduction

Glimmerings I is the first volume of a collection of thoughts and observations spanning forty years of my life. I do not remember what made me begin to write down my ideas, and some of the early ones make me wonder. Perhaps it was the desire that sometime in the future my children or grandchildren would profit by my life experience and wisdom. Perhaps it was plain vanilla egotism in thinking that I knew something wise to say.

My philosophy about wisdom is that it should be gained, used, and shared. Growing wise without applying the wisdom would mean that one had not really grown wise. Not sharing the wisdom would be selfish and, um, unwise. Of the three purposes, I hope I have gained some wisdom (you can be the judge), and I hope I sometimes use it. But, whatever the state of the first two, at least here I have fulfilled the purpose of sharing what I have thought worth passing along.

I first read Marcus Aurelius' *Meditations* in 1979, Blaise Pascal's *Pensees* in 1980, and Dag Hammarskjold's *Markings* in 1992. Had I read these before I started, I would eagerly credit them with the idea of starting my own notebook. At any rate, I recommend that you, O reader, consider carefully taking up the pen or keyboard and noting down whatever you learn from your experiences that might profit those who have yet to tread the path you have already taken.

I've inserted an occasional date, together with my age at the time, so that you can say, "This is what he thought when he was X years old." At the time, I thought each idea was worth noting for future reference or enlightenment. If some of the ideas appear quaint, wrong, or silly, I can always claim that I might have matured out of them.

This volume contains the first 1001 Glimmerings that I wrote, from 1974 at age 23 through 1982 at age 31. If you enjoy these and want to read the second volume, containing another 1001 Glimmerings, you'll see that they were written from age 23 to 63. I guess I've been slowing down.

One small note: For many years these entries were called *Light Bulbs of Various Wattages*. It was the best title I could think of at age 23, and I still think of the entries as light bulbs. But I thought a title with better resonance would be preferable, so I chose *Glimmerings* to reflect my hope that the entries would offer some light on the topic they addressed.

Just as Marcus Aurelius' book is literally titled *To Himself*, so the *you* in these entries should be understood as referring to me, talking to myself. I keep trying to teach myself something. If you gain a tidbit of wisdom by overhearing, so much the better.

Because most of the entries are short, you can keep this book handy for those idle moments when you want to grab an idea to chew on. Short bits should suit very well an age that has no time for protracted indulgence in philosophical writings. These you can eat like potato chips. Chomp one and savor its flavor. When you have time or inclination, chomp another. And remember, all philosophy is valued not so much for having the right answers as for asking the right questions, introducing an idea or a novel approach to an idea, suggesting a line of thinking, provoking reexamination of a concept, or even being wrong in interesting ways. I hope you will enter here with that attitude. And, of course, when you realize that I really am right and astute and profound, you will remark what a clever and wise person I am.

Glimmerings

[Circa 1974; about age 23]

1. Rain water runs down tree bark channels in Pine, Oak, Red-wood, etc. and is slowed in flow—speed and violence broken. Water is delivered non-erosively to the base of the tree, its roots, and nearby seedlings.

2. How different is the sound of a burned over forest—no rush-ing movement or sound of air through gently agitated tree tops—no birds chirping—just eerie stillness and hollow wind sound or silence altogether. The acoustics have changed and changed our mood with them. The ground under the trees is all gray black dirt—the needles, leaves, bark, grasses, flowers, have all vanished—turned to a uniform powder. You look at the for-est and see through it. You can see too far, and it strikes you as not right. Before, you looked at the forest and saw a few feet into the greenery, then no farther—the forest was revealed to you gradually as you walked through it. Now you have an al-most unobstructed view across hills and down valleys—seems as if you can see miles—the only obstructions are gray rocks and skeletal trees—and they all now look just alike. The trees stand there with their dead arms outstretched, and they don't look right.

3. We must have Axe-head Lake and Oak Tree Lake.

4. The crackling of a fire in the fireplace. The hot coals.

5. Pursue knowledge but seek wisdom.

6. Add the water of life to our dust and we become the clay the Lord can work to his mind—to make of us what he will. The clay is fired by the tribulations of life, so we can become the final, sturdy, useful vessel.

7. We like to go to the seashore and watch the waves because of their limitless energy. The pounding waves never tire—beating rhythmically against the sand and rocks. We also sense their power—probably the feeling from those heavy, low vibrations—such power as that (like that of a strong wind) always inspires us.

8. Man needs woman as a tempering influence on the male passions, angers, tendency to distrust, and skeptical outlook. God created woman as a helper for man, and so she should be.

9. Whether it is worse to kill the body or to torture the soul.

10. Question: How does one determine class? Answer: Class is determined by how far the bedroom is from the front door.

11. How many tourists have discovered that magazine glossies are not true "pictures" of reality?

12. One problem we constantly face in a mass media society is the popular confusion of fame with merit or intelligence. A well-known columnist, "personality," star, newsman, or politician is not necessarily worthy of imitation or praise. In fact, in many cases, famous people are the most dense, short sighted, corrupt, bigoted, unlearned folks you'd ever hope to avoid if you were able. Knowledge, wisdom, and virtue should be sought in every area of society—without much regard to fame. Somehow those chosen to become famous have only that to recommend them.

13. Beware of intellectual Pavlov reactions. Keep your mind

open to new arguments on old topics. Don't assume that everyone who believes "A" also believes "B." Be careful lest you misrepresent your opponents or begin to use *ad hominem* arguments.

14. A minister is to be the spiritual leader of his church; as such he should not act informally or like a "pal" from the pulpit. When preaching he should present himself in a sober, solemn, worshipful manner. There is room for the expression of Godly joy in song and prayer, but the minister should avoid cracking jokes, or giving the impression that his work is a game. He should do nothing that would in any way lessen the dignity of his office and his calling.

15. Woman is too quick to change, man too slow. Woman, by and large, is driven by every flight of fancy and every whim, to shift her ground. Man, when he once seizes upon a belief, whether through careful thought or sudden choice, is often extremely stubborn in maintaining it, even to the exclusion of contrary evidence or rational refutation of his idea. Obviously, the more carefully thought out and formulated positions should require (and withstand) much more contrary argumentation to overcome them. But we find that usually those who hold the most bigoted stances have the least backing or reasoning supporting them.

16. Art is not meant to be a box-camera snapshot of reality.

17. There is no situation, however bad it may be (outside the most excruciating physical pain), that cannot to a great degree be improved or made more bearable by one's own mental and spiritual powers. Your outlook or attitude is important. Face disappointments and failures, and contrary events with cheer and courage, asking God's help and trusting in him, and these problems will be much lighter than you imagined. By allowing your problems to feed upon yourself, on the other hand, they will consume you. Surprise.

18. Every disaster in your life is not the end of the world, so you should not act so. The end of the world will come only once, and then it will be too late to mourn.

19. If you fight against yourself, you are pitching two armies, of which one will seldom if ever get the better of the other, yet continue to fight. They both draw their supplies from the same source—you. All your energy will soon be used, you will be worn out, and no real battle has been fought.

20. What is it that possesses some women to run the mouth constantly at full speed without ever engaging the brain?

21. The biggest problem with people in relation to poor results is the general lack of competence. This is due largely to ignorance and unwillingness to learn. The second biggest problem is the unwillingness to persevere or to do a thorough job. People are too quick to say they can't find it (and then give up) or they can't do it (and then give up) or they will do a half-hearted job and declare that that is good enough. Look a little harder, try a little longer, and do your best in everything. Make effort and quality important factors.

22. Here's a tribute to the energy of waitresses during the dinner hour.

23. The sun may go down, but the light shall not go out until my labor is advanced.

24. Discrimination is the basis for every value we have. That one thing is to be preferred over another, that one thing is better or worse than another, is the sum of the philosophy behind quality, standards, progress, and excellence.

25. It seems an almost inescapable law of nature that rapid technological advancement comes best when there is a group of

small firms in an industry. Too large a capital outlay is required for a very expansive corporation to change its current production machinery: one new bit and one new tape feed cost less in total (though perhaps not in percentage) than a thousand of each. And often only the vicious snapping of that mutt competition (the consumer's pet) at the heels of industry will persuade a particular corporation to adventure some money on an experiment to move it ahead. It is simple physics to say the larger the corporate mass, the more inertia to change there will be, and the greater momentum to roll in the same direction there is. And it is simple observation to say that fat ladies to not dance as lithely as slender ones. Remember how many inventions were brought into being by one man playing in his basement or garage, and then developed and marketed by him also.

26. Wisdom is the selection, organization, and abstraction of knowledge, which produces sound judgments and correct discernments between *true* and *false*. It is the practical and philosophical *application* of knowledge or learning; and since it deals with application, it cannot be learned directly, as from a book. Thought, deduction, and experience (at least of a vicarious nature) are required.

27. A certain amount of tolerance is not only good but necessary also for the proper and efficient functioning of the social machine. Too much tolerance in any part, however, causes noise, structural fatigue, excess wear, vibration, leakage, or all of these, and will almost certainly result in the inevitable, even if eventual, failure of the entire machine. And as the tolerance increases, either through sloppy allowances or through constant wear, the rapidity of the failure increases also. But it should be remembered that too little tolerance prevents the machine from running at all, or makes its labor so strained that no work can be done. Finally, without the lubricants of Christian morality and reason, even an otherwise well adjusted social machine will be quickly ruined.

28. In order for something concrete to flow out of the brain, a little external cement must be added to the congenital sand-and-water mix in the head. Otherwise, you must hope it never rains on your intellectual castles—and this in a season when the dark clouds of criticism and argument loom everywhere.

29. To act for good in silence is to act alone; for who likes to do anything of worth without calling out loudly for attention to it? Many are ready to be quiet when performing their wickednesses, and to suppress them thereafter, but to say nothing when by speaking up one could receive praise—have his ego pumped—and perhaps gather some material reward, well, that is asking too much.

30. Remember God in your prosperity and he will not forget you in your need.

31. The mind is like a pool of water where ideas and knowledge must flow in and out in order to maintain freshness and purity. If nothing flows in, the pool will dry up; if nothing flows out, it will stagnate.

32. Every gift is capable of use and misuse. There is no gift or talent, however noble, that cannot be used for the most vile and wicked purposes; nor is there any gift or talent, however humble, but can be used for the edification of men, the sanctification of the believer, and the great glory of God.

33. Many people like to prolong their crises—to wallow in their plight—and therefore won't readily accept a simple or immediate solution. They must worry and complain awhile first. They, in fact, seem to discuss and describe their woes, and complain about them, not to receive a solution, but to get sympathy.

34. How is he? Let's put it this way—his soul is packing its suitcase.

35. All free men, subject to God's will, are arbiters of their own destinies. No man is compelled to subject himself to the petty dictates of some puerile despot as long as there is a higher level of government which remains untyrannical. When the dictates of an employer or a municipality, for example, become unbearable, the victim is at liberty to move. At times it becomes necessary to sacrifice convenience and preference to freedom: While the farmer's abundant grain may be preferable to the thinly scattered wild grasses of the distant hillsides, his heavy yoke has from the Creation prevented the beasts of the field from volunteering their services.

36. Greed seldom or never prospers, for it causes such a selfish and perverse behavior that it drives away cooperation, friendship, and generosity; it causes such an overbearing and grasping attitude that it offends those whom the greedy would court—such as his customers or those from whom he would like service.

37. Why do men forsake the water that would wash off the mud of the world? Is it because they realize that once they bathe, they cannot put their old clothes back on? Or because they think the new clothes (which have no tears or holes) will be less comfortable? Or is it the Comfort of Mud they cannot forsake?

38. The phrase, "innocent until proven guilty," should be understood only with regard to the state. Justice is said to be blind because the state pretends not to have seen or been aware of the crime prior to its disclosure in court. The person on trial either committed the crime or he didn't. If he shot someone over network TV, or there were lots of witnesses, etc., he is surely guilty before the trial begins. But the state considers his guilt unproven (i.e., he is "innocent" temporarily) until it is established in court. The purpose of a trial is to determine guilt to the satisfaction of the state, and to decide upon what action should be taken against the defendant, if any. The important thing to remember is that the state *never* finds anyone "innocent." The non-

convicting verdict is "not guilty," which simply means that not enough evidence has been brought forth to prove a suspect guilty. This does not mean he did not commit the crime. A person who is an admitted, witnessed criminal, though let off by a court, may in all propriety still be referred to as a "guilty criminal" by the layman.

39. There are some cowards hiding behind the mask of title and the shield of position, who occasionally venture out for a moment to attack their own men, but who never muster enough courage to fight the enemy in the real world. The underlings or employees of these men granted power past their capabilities are most to be pitied, for they must fight on two fronts. They are like a nation at war, which is at the same time torn by civil discord from within.

40. Yes, I recall what you said yesterday, but I thought that surely by now your brain would catch up with your mouth and you'd have reconsidered.

[Summer, 1975; age 24]

41. Education is a hard road to drive. One must keep alert for the curves and hard places, miss the pot holes of false teaching, and stay on the right side of the road through the fogs of discord and the glaring headlights of opposition. But it is a satisfying trip nevertheless. The smooth road of ignorance is all a boring sameness, conducive to laxity and sleep. And it leads nowhere.

42. If there were any other boat in the sea of atheism, the passengers would abandon the ship of evolution like rats leaving a sinking garbage barge.

43. Now—a completely new and surprising edition of the Holy Bible, updated, rewritten, and translated in light of the latest modern discoveries, theories, and popular notions. Get yours

today.

44. The judgment of a work of art in its time is usually errone-ous, unless done by those possessing the perspective of histori-cal evaluation and the knowledge of true quality.

45. A question much obscured recently is: should a president (or any elected official) do what is right, or what the majority of those who elected him wish him to do?

46. Why is a satire considered fiction when it is the truest form of all?

47. One of God's best gifts to woman is her ability to act inter-ested, ask questions, and listen to a man talk for a long time, when she doesn't really care at all about anything he is saying. This listening benefits the man not merely because he feels he is "being interesting to a woman" (thus elevating his self esteem), but more importantly, it allows him to clarify his own thoughts on a matter: "He seeth how they looke when they are turned into Words" as Francis Bacon puts it in "Of Friendship." Now, if only the woman were *really* interested, and needed no dis-simulation. . . .

48. Whom God loves, must I not love also?

49. A plant—a weed—is a living organism with complex func-tioning biological processes. It contains intricate clocks, measur-ing devices, detectors. It somehow knows bloom time, relative moisture levels, sunshine intensity and direction. The plant manufactures and processes, increases in size, establishes equi-libriums (hundred-foot-tall trees are perfectly balanced); it re-produces itself. And an animal does all these things—and moves. And man thinks about them and glorifies God.

50. There's no substitute for knowledge, not even experience.

51. I would think just the memory of the follies one has indulged in the past would serve to make one careful and temperate in his actions, but apparently this is not so.

52. A pessimist resists every success and welcomes every failure. He sees successes as small or ordinary, nothing to be happy about; failures he sees as confirmations of his dark outlook, and therefore as friends. Men should not be that way. Change what inequities you can and don't worry inordinately about the rest. Most of all, don't harp continually about things—"injustices" which neither you nor your hearers can remedy. Such talk only makes the room stuffy and the occupants uneasy.

53. Where good men prosper and the bad receive their just desserts.

54. Advertising and fadmania are responsible for the ridiculous notions that, by definition, old is bad and new is good. What exactly, is Old Fashioned? Is that when they used metal instead of plastic and rivets instead of glue?

55. Think of the books on your shelf—each one waiting patiently to speak to you when you would give attention. A stored treasure which will still be witty and fresh after ten years of your neglect, as it has remained so after hundreds of years of other men's neglect. Think how much knowledge, study, pains, and thought are represented by a foot or two of your shelf. And think of a library, where the quintessence of thousands of minds rests together ready to enlighten any man who cares enough to read.

56. All proscriptive law is legislated morality. It is a set of rules which forms the operative basis of society, and permits an orderly, safe, and profitable interaction among men. The cornerstone of every civilization rests upon the codified (and guaranteed) moral behavior of its citizens. Without such proper guarantees, every social act must be undertaken with fear and dis-

trust, governed by suspicion, and concluded with haste.

57. Three R's which should be taught in addition to the standard ones are Restraint, Rectitude, and Righteousness.

58. A dictionary according to usage is what's commonly known as codified ignorance.

59. We must strive for the active realization that man's ephemeral acts have eternal consequences.

60. The sound of horses' hoofs on cobblestones at night.

61. Like an old man, who, having spent his life vainly searching the barren deserts for wealth, finally discovers a tiny fleck of gold, and dies in the excitement of his find.

62. Her naked feet softly crushing the tufts of grass.

63. And you sink into a doubtful twilight, in an unthought evening fallen. But do you repent?

64. Don't be so proud, don't be so sensitive; in a word, don't take yourself so seriously.

65. When Socrates said, "Know Thyself," he did not mean that one should seek out his own ego and overinflate it, priding oneself in all the wonderful qualities and accomplishments he pretends to possess or to have attained. Socrates probably meant that one should constantly scrutinize himself for errors, faults, and shortcomings, with an eye toward correction and improvement. If we look inward and examine ourselves, we will almost certainly find the condition known in the real estate business as "deferred maintenance." Perhaps it is time to make a few repairs.

66. Why are people so sensitive to their own feelings and so cal-

lous toward the rest of the world?

67. The fewer pretensions we have, the more room there will be in our hearts for something genuine.

68. Just as no one realizes the convenience and utility of a *drain* until it backs up.

[January, 1976; age 25]

69. Strive to love, and know, and be on good terms with God in both success and failure, victory and defeat, happiness and sorrow. Loving God only when you are happy or prosperous, and seeking his guidance and help only in distresses, shows a shallow and selfish soul. Trust him, instead of your wretched, groveling self.

70. Knowledge makes men cautious. It is easy to deceive ignorance because they who are unknowing are not cautious, even when they profess to be highly suspicious. They will swallow professed truth with little encouragement. Yet once a particular notion has been formed in this way, no amount of truth or argument or demonstration will sway or correct them. Advice: Don't disbelieve all you hear, but check it, or seek a confirming opinion before fixing it permanently in your mind. Don't reject every new stone out of hand, but check it for cracks, feel its weight with your own hands, and try it for fit before cementing it forever into the superstructure of your understanding. And should you find sometime that one of your rocks of fact or truth was only a clay impostor, don't be afraid to chip it out and repair the breach. The sign of a magnanimous soul is the willingness to correct mistakes rather than to deny them.

71. With reference to Glimmering #16, on Art: Painting will never be superseded by photography, because painting (1) collects objects which we cannot find together in nature, (2) can heighten, emphasize, and obscure objects in ways untouchable

by a photographer, (3) can perfect or corrupt objects in representation while the photographer must be pretty well content with what he sees, having only light and angle at his disposal, and (4) the painter can invent landscapes, persons, clothes, etc. which do not exist at all.

72. It's easy to attack objections to small things as trivial, but it is the small things that make a happy (or unhappy) society. People are unhappier in today's society, and it is more corrupt than in former days because of so many small, antisocial crimes. People butt in line more—it won't alter the course of civilization perhaps, but it will have an effect. The resentment of those offended will be expressed somewhere against other members of the community. People steal little things, tell small lies, break convenience laws (like no parking here, etc.), speak little insults. Look at the way people dress now—they just don't care how they look to others—and this not caring about others is why we as a society are decaying.

73. The people who get the most emotionally strained over an issue often have a guilty conscience to defend.

74. There is little to be desired materially in life besides a good library, ice water, and an amiable wife. To which I would add, if pressed, some classical records, some fine art, and an electric blanket. If pressed further, I might admit to cheese, white wine, Twenties' films, and peanuts. Not to mention air conditioning.

75. There is little more dangerous than angered ignorance.

76. The counterparts of #74 create the formula for a life of misery and despair: bad books, tap water, a disagreeable wife, rock music, modern art—you'd better keep the electric blanket with a disagreeable wife—gallon jug red wine, modern movies, and—gasp—no cheese or peanuts. Not to mention no air conditioning.

77. How often do you go outside at night and look at the stars?

78. Not time, but knowledge, makes an expert.

79. How little time out of our lives is actually spent in serving or praising God. And this is how we choose to have our eternal rewards measured unto us.

80. No one, except the government, can spend money he doesn't have.

81. The evils of man are summed up in that current phrase, "I want your body now": *I* reveals the pride and egotism of man; *want*, his greed and selfishness; *your*, his envy and covetousness; *body*, his lust and carnal temperament; *now*, his foolish urgency and impatience about everything.

82. Too many people cultivate offensive sensitivity; that is, they perfect the art of being offended easily—on the slightest (or nonexistent) provocation. People should instead cultivate receptive sensitivity; that is, the capability of being moved emotionally, spiritually, and intellectually by the beauties of nature, the successes of art, the happy turns of literature and music, etc. How many exquisite blades of grass, and neat expressions are passed by because of the insensitivity—the callousness—of men?

83. What is worse than the misery of him who views every ordinary occurrence in his life as humdrum, and every unusual event as a crisis?

84. The tender song of an owl, backed by the orchestration of crickets, adds an unsurpassable richness to a balmy, still night.

85. As pure as crystal, but as true as steel.

86. Why do your eyes leak water when you're unhappy?

87. The general happiness and well-being of society is directly related to and dependent upon freedom. Freedom is directly related to and mainly dependent upon the property right. "All property depends upon the chastity of women." Therefore, the general happiness and well-being of society is directly related to and mainly dependent upon the chastity of women.

88. How morally corrupt has our society become that we must now put nipples on mannequins?

89. Women are somehow possessed with an innate desire to talk, without regard to the presence or absence of a subject. . . .

90. Ah! what a piece of work is woman: created by the hand of God as a multiple-use helper and companion to man. How happy was the Lord's intent to make this creature, and how delightful is a proper specimen — perfect in conception, wonderful in design, and exquisite in the execution. And how fallen are the others.

91. The job of a college professor is to point the way with his finger, not lead the student by his hand.

92. How frequently do the same things occur over and over again in life. May we prepare ourselves for future encores the first time we meet an event. May we prepare for the original event the first time we suspect it.

93. It doesn't make sense to us, but look who we are.

94. Sunshine and Flame.

95. No one praises the Lord that I exist, and that is a very great difference.

96. Take evolution for example. I don't think man's knowledge,

or scholarship, or happiness, or virtue is increased by having this theory; no genuine curiosity is satisfied, no order of reason is created, no useful tool is given—so what good is it? It is merely an excuse to avoid God and escape the claims of Christ. So many theories seem likewise useless scientifically because generated only for philosophical comfort. We want truth, not tickled ears.

97. Why should "rich" people not only be subject to a percentage tax, but also be punished by a graduated percentage tax? Answer: Because they have more money and are better able to pay. —Very good. So the next time you want to buy a TV we will charge you fifty dollars more than Jones here (who makes less than you do) because you are "better able to pay." After all, a "rich man" is anyone who makes more money than you do, right?

98. A widespread, irrational prejudice about a particular item, person, or genre, is known as *mystique*.

99. What if something happens? —Well, what if the sun burns out and nobody notices?

100. A Christian is he who subscribes his name to the roll of believers in the fulfilling life, substitutionary death, and life-giving resurrection of the Lord Jesus Christ, the Son of God.

101. It is striking to observe how many people are vainly racing against Time, who, by the way, is never himself in a hurry; even so, he wins nearly all of his races because no man can match his endurance. Besides, he has, if I may say so, all the time in the world.

102. Thine is the day, and the night is Thine.

103. Predictability is an extremely important and desirable characteristic in any person. Francis Bacon says to men in his

essay, "Of Great Place," "Seeke to make thy Course Regular; that Men may know before hand what they may expect," but I would enlarge this advice to apply to bosses, teachers, spouses, friends—indeed, to everyone who wishes others to obey, love, trust, or respect him. Happiness depends upon your predictability. An unexpected action or reaction in a person of close relationship or power causes a highly detrimental surprise and shock effect on the part of the friend or underling. Some claim to like unpredictable people, for the excitement and novelty, they say, but a lasting relationship cannot be built on such a foundation. It is like playing with fire—fun, but uncomfortable or nerve wracking, or tension building. A predictable person allows planning and directed effort, while giving security to the emotions and a sense of stability—both in the friend and in the predictable person himself. And the predictable person is not stagnant or boring; rather his energies are pointed and ordered. While the unpredictable person grows in every direction, like a bush, the predictable person grows in a single direction like a giant redwood tree: every side shoot is reasonable and unsurprising, and serves ultimately to add height and bulk to the main trunk, as it reaches for the skies.

104. Fleeting sexual thoughts should not bother you excessively. It is no sin to find a renegade in your house if you throw him out the door. But when you greet him with a smile, ask him to stay, entertain him, fatten him up, and invite his friends, then you have sinned.

105. Almighty God, grant us forgiveness for the sins we perform unwillingly and in times of weakness; turn not from us with just indignation; but supply us with strength to turn from evil and to resist further temptations. This do for Jesus' sake, Amen.

106. We must come to the realization that there are indeed people who love wickedness and evil more than good, and falsehood more than truth.

107. When clouds have blown and all the bundled heat has fled.

108. People are always worried about their intelligence. Don't worry about how smart you are, but worship and serve God to the best of your abilities. Let us suppose you are absolutely the dumbest person in the world. God will not love you the less; and if you serve him to the best of your abilities, your reward will not be any less than that of the smartest person in the world who does likewise. And you are still capable of the pleasures of learning and knowledge, even if they don't make you a great thinker or an intellectual. Learning will make up a lot for any supposed lack of native intelligence. [margin:] Retarded people and mental patients are often among the kindest and gentlest people.

109. Art room accidents, street garbage, cultural promiscuity. The tears of reflective, conquered innocence.

110. Those who concentrate on the sexual aspect of females sometimes forget there is no *b* in *woman*. That is, man's helper is not "womban."

111. Wisdom won't save you. God will save you, if you believe. Wise men die.

112. Ask her, "Are you everything I should desire in a woman?"

113. Pride *must* be conquered through submission. See Matthew 11:28-30.

114. Be and seek a person of internal steadfastness who has resistance to fads and group pressure, and who seeks God's will and *trusts* him. This is the same quality that makes a strong and enduring faith — perhaps "the firm root in himself" of Matthew 13:21. "We are the trees whom shaking fastens more." — Herbert

115. Two bodies stationary will never find each other; two bodies moving, seldom; one stationary and one moving, eventually.

116. It is not necessary, or even desirable, to have an opinion about everything.

117. Mark Twain—the man who tried to make friends with the devil.

118. The book, I do not doubt, is Meaningful; but whether it is full of meaning only the true test of time will tell.

119. Women should not confuse the expression of their intelligence with aggression. A woman who is genuine must not pretend to be ignorant or incapable when she is not—the usual case—but neither should she pretend to be informed or able when she is not. Falseness of every kind is eventually discovered, and as it sows the seeds of thistles, prickly weeds are the only result. "They are neither to wonder nor repine, when a contract begun with fraud has ended in disappointment." — Johnson, *Rambler* 45.

120. God grant us the stability we need to persevere.

121. All art is representative art. If the work does not represent something in the natural or human world in a pictorial or directly imitative sense, it will at least represent the state and condition of the artist's mind and soul.

122. All recurring taxes upon property are evil.

123. Good music should be listened to in a dark or dimly lit room, preferably alone, and with your eyes closed. If you can find a kindred spirit and listen unselfconsciously and *without talking*, that is okay. You should listen at a time when you will not be interrupted. Good music flows into the soul.

124. For someone to think himself wonderful for any reason at all is the height of egotism, but for someone to think himself wonderful because of his biological nature — his race or sex — is the height of absurdity.

125. It is upsetting when the media, professors, or persons quoted act as if everyone cultured or intelligent or aware or reasonable now subscribes to the particular opinion they are promoting. They further imply that the only people opposing them are kooks, retards, no-counts, fanatics, etc.

126. Professors often refuse to believe in anything because they think this makes them intellectual. "After all, there are surely arguments against everything." These profs refuse to pin down or get involved in certain moral issues, and practice only the usual "me too" liberal politics. "He was teaching them as one having authority, and not as their professors." — Matt. 7:29 (Doax Version)

127. Another problem with professors — and people in general — is the "Appeal to Superman" fallacy. This takes the form of appealing to a vague or non-existent higher authority who is knowledgeable in some field the disputant is not. For example, "Well of course the Logicians could shoot holes in that." "The Historians have shown that so and so is the case" — or worse — "The Historians *could* prove you are wrong."

128. There is a penalty for being good or virtuous in this world, and a penalty for having good taste. Expediency and immorality speed many to the top; the virtuous must be content with less — in this world. Amorality — the eyes and mouth closed syndrome, or the "don't oppose anything too much, be a chum(p), eh what" attitude — also raises the fool to a higher place. Good taste is expensive in books. So few people buy them — the editions of the good old rich books — that the price must be very high to cover costs. Bad books are sold in such quantities that a paperback is quickly available for a pittance.

Then, too, people will pay more for bad books. And, of course, the more evil a book is, the more publicity it receives, and the more copies it sells.

129. The poetry of the 16th century is fresh milk.
The poetry of the 17th century is rich cream.
The poetry of the 18th century is tangy cranberry juice.
The poetry of the 19th century is sugary Kool-Aid.
The poetry of the 20th century is water of suspicious origin.

130. These professors who act as if it is such a big concession to the cosmos on their part because they will admit to belief in God—they will allow him to exist out of their magnanimity—make me want to puke. The devil believes in God, and he's not even a professor.

131. I will pursue a course of composition such that future generations will say of me, "He made Swift look like a philanthropist."

132. "Woe to you, teachers and professors, hypocrites, because you travel about on sea and land to get one graduate student, and when he becomes one, you make him twice as much a son of hell as yourselves." —Matt. 23:15 (Doax Version)

"Woe to you, teachers and professors, hypocrites, because you shut off the kingdom of heaven from your students, for you do not enter in yourselves; nor do you allow those who are entering to go in." —Matt. 23:13 (Doax Version)

133. A single dose of Experiment is often sufficient to put the wandering of Speculation back into the sphere of Reality.

134. Please submit an exact approximation.

135. If the world will not accept the slashings of my razor, I shall lay it down and take up my sledge hammer.

136. Certain things deserve more fame than others.
Certain things deserve more fame than they now have.
Certain things deserve less fame that they now have.

137. To destroy does not commonly mean to annihilate. Rather it means to alienate from an original or natural function. Thus in the context of a destroyed car, or as in Matthew 10:28, a destroyed soul, the object is rendered useless, but not put out of existence.

138. One of the fundamental lessons of life is to realize that we cannot read hearts. It is a very grave error to imagine we can discover the feelings of another by his outward behavior or demeanor. Those who hurt the most often show it least.

139. There are intellectual pleasures, physical pleasures, and those in between or overlapping. For example, it gives some men pleasure to turn bolts with a wrench. This is a physical act which, in some measure at least, gives intellectual satisfaction.

140. Pray for God's will. If you pray for your own, your prayer may be answered — to your horror.

141. The great mistake of the Romantic artists is that they record their emotions. The job of an artist as it touches the realm of feeling is to *create* emotion, not to record it. Of course, the Romantics are also astray in their exclusive concern with emotion, their cultivation of the ego, their denial of absolutes, and their hatred of the intellect.

142. By their refusal to make quality discriminations, the egalitarians have sabotaged their own ideals. They first wanted everyone to be equally educated. The hard subjects discriminated against the less bright, so those subjects were eased or thrown out, and everything easy or meaningless or fun was permitted in the name of education. Now the university degree has been reduced to the level of every man — it is a social certificate,

backed by an unstructured or anarchic process of pretend-learning; students are indeed taught the "idle notions and babblements" Milton asserts. And the typical student emerges in the most dangerous of all states: ignorant, bigoted, and egotistical. "A little learning is a dangerous thing."

143. The plot of a story serves as a hook on which to hang the communications of the author to the reader, in what the characters say and do, and, very occasionally, in authorial comments (18th century style). But the plot is also a means in itself for communication, when taken as a whole. The movement of events, the success or failure of virtuous or vicious characters, the places described, and the events which pass without comment, all serve to convey a message. There is no such thing as no comment. When nothing is emphasized, it implies that nothing deserves emphasis; when nothing is praised or condemned, it implies that nothing deserves praise or condemnation. Simple description can be telltale: is the world viewed as a meaningless slum or as a place of hope and opportunity?

144. Perhaps the gnawing belief in the heart of many that evolution is not science has spurred the current frantic search for life on other planets—the main reason for our entire space program. Much more money seems to be spent on apparatus to discover traces of life than on any other kind of data collection equipment.

145. Fully the half of knowledge consists in asking the right questions. Progress is often better served by asking a new question than by seeking a new answer to an old question.

146. The beginning place for emotional and psychological well being is consistency. Remember that equanimity is no more than the assurance of direction amidst the threat of chaos.

147. A single basic attitude is responsible for much of the technical greatness of this nation. The first Americans entered the

country with very little; what European technology they had was not completely adequate. There was a need for innovation, and whatever the challenge, the American was willing to try. By the continuing willingness to take a chance and try something new, and by the willingness of the government to keep out of the way and to allow new things to be tried, we have risen to the status of the greatest technical power of the world. The other nations of the world, with longer histories, traditions, and habits of government regulation, were not able to match us. But now we too have an interfering government and established ways of doing and making things; large corporations are now hesitant to try the new or to take a chance — after all, it is costly, and it may not work, and the government may not allow it. I pity the person or company that is not willing to fail, for they will never succeed. Not a readiness to succeed but a readiness to fail is the key to all progress.

148. Many are concerned with the various steps this nation should take to insure that justice will be dispensed to all. But few ask the basic question which is a necessary beginning for all such inquiries. The question is, Why should we have justice, even supposing a definition can be agreed upon? For what reason should there be "equal justice under law"? The answer cannot be, as some would assert, that such is the will of the people or that we must promote the greatest good for the greatest number; for such concepts lead inevitably not only to a tyranny of the majority but even to conditions such as those in Nazi Germany, where the greatest good was promoted as a plan to exterminate an entire racial group. Additionally, a particular act of justice may be highly displeasing to a majority of the people. Why should there be justice? Because God has *commanded* us to be just, according to his objective standard; happiness is only a by product, not a motive.

149. Man has not yet mastered the art of singing loud praises and serving in silent humility.

150. If the chirping of a cricket be granted as a praise to God, what an insect is man, who is not merely unwilling himself to sing to the skies, but must happily crush the life out of the creature who does.

151. Where a law is not enforced, it does not exist.

152. It is defeat rather than success that most sharpens our abilities.

153. The single most important quality in a wife is not beauty, vivacity, personality, culture, or even intellect or consistency; it is loyalty.

154. Should we but once have a law requiring the first person pronouns to be emphasized whenever they are used, perhaps it would put each person on notice how much his own ego runs amok in the course of a day. "Excuse *me*, but *I* think you are in *my* way."

155. The shooting star receives momentary acclaim, and is forgotten; the shining star whose brightness is reliable and consistent is perpetually remarked. *Consistent* excellence is more important to the advancement and happiness of mankind than a momentary explosion of unequalable glory.

156. With reference to Glimmering #153, the second most important quality in a wife is congeniality—the happy agreeableness which greatly eases the burden of life.

157. Where minimal care will long preserve a thing (whether object or relationship), minimal neglect will quickly render it useless or inoperative.

158. A careless attitude is second only to wanton destruction.

159. When you must cheat to win, there is glory in losing.

160. The disgruntled egotist who feels the world is handing him a bad deal must learn that each person makes his own deals; the world hands nothing to anybody. If you wait for the world to right the supposed wrongs it has dealt you, you'll die in your chair—with a very sore behind. Accept the blame for your own mistakes and don't allow the mistakes of the past to hinder you. Repent and pursue a new direction.

161. Well son, life can't always be a bowl full of cherries; now sit down and eat your peaches and cream.

162. If the energy, determination, persistence, and sacrifice of the athlete could be directed toward a more valuable and lasting goal (for example, spiritual, moral, or intellectual improvement of which every man could partake and share in the success), what wonders might arise; what a pushing back of the frontiers of knowledge we would have, what gains in wisdom, and what health of spirit we could achieve.

163. No man is more cruel, or more to be pitied, than he who loses the desire to please.

[Summer, 1976; age 25]

164. **Lessons learned from watching the Games of the 21st Olympiad:**
    1. Consistency and repeatability are more important than freak peaking. The ability to perform on demand is the mark of a champion. (See also, Glimmering #155.)
    2. One must be goal-directed to succeed. Any wandering or uncertainty will delay or end your project. Know exactly what you want to accomplish and how you intend to go about it; *then* begin.
    3. Many barriers are very strong, but the world is malleable, and very little in it will not yield to energy, determination, persistence, and sacrifice. The man who will in every case keep try-

ing for ten minutes after all others have quit, will soon rule the world.

4. Sometimes the real winners in a contest, the non-cheating winners, do not finish first, and must wait for their due recognition.

165. Pleasure without responsibility is always degenerative.

166. Most people, and nations, get what they deserve, because they get what they ask for.

167. The purpose of duty is to continue virtue when the warmth of fervid adherence has cooled. We have a duty toward truth and an obligation toward justice. Currently there is little warmth of sentiment toward either.

168. In the learning of some lessons, the price of experience is too high; in such cases we learn vicariously from the admonitions of our elders, who have either themselves paid the price of experience, or know of someone who has.

169. It used to be that the purpose of literature was to teach and to entertain — *dulce et utile.* Then literature became merely a source of idle dissipation. Now it fulfills the role of a psychic torture apparatus, generating mental and emotional problems.

170. The adolescent frequently suffers from ego problems because he has not yet learned that pride is an enemy, and that self seeking can never lead to happiness or fulfillment. "Nobody cares that I'm alive," he says; and mopes about it, when the answer he needs is, "So what?" As Johnson notes in *Rambler* 146, only a few people at most care about the life of any particular person, and sometimes even that care is more or less selfish. God cares that you are alive and he cares what you do; that should be your entire concern. See the eleventh paragraph of *Rambler* 185. And yet, the need for human love is very real.

171. The job of the academic critic is not to offer his own silly gut reactions to a piece of literature, but to explicate its meaning and fill in needed historical background. His job is to condense his pertinent learning into textual footnotes and a useful introduction. Clarification of difficult or obscure passages, explanations of allusions, definitions of rare or strange words, and some remarks on influences, traditions, genres, etc. are his main concern. Performing a competent job on these items is enough to keep any scholar busy. This information given to the reader is what enriches the literature; the critic's own opinions on psychology or verve only make the reader bored or queasy.

172. All taxation of pure capital is evil—e.g., real estate, inheritance, and vehicle registration (based on value) taxes. All graduated taxes are evil, too. It's bad enough to pay a percentage rather than a fixed sum.

173. Selling the kitchen to the wife sells the house.

174. Think—it may be your last chance.

175. Thought is like childbirth: it is painful in the process, but results in a permanently cherished offspring.

176. To a beginning thinker—one who would give up musing for real thinking—the labor of thought is very difficult. With time and practice it will grow easier and more natural, but it will always require effort.

177. While thought will always be hard, it will always be rewarding.

178. Each day, think and pray on these things:
   Morning: In your prayers give thanks. In your thoughts think on
      1) What you can do this day to improve yourself.
      2) Your faith and your soul's health.

3) What you can do for the propagation of the gospel.

Noon: In your prayers ask guidance. In your thoughts think on

1) Your personal virtue expressed in thought and deed.

2) The uselessness of pride and vanity.

3) The transitoriness of all things worldly.

Night: In your prayers ask forgiveness. In your thoughts think on

1) Your ultimate, if not immediate, death.

2) Your actions of the day and the effect they will have on yourself and on others.

3) The repair of your soul for the sins of the day.

179. It is general unwillingness to learn, rather than a general inability, which hinders the progress of mankind.

180. Unscrubbed bodies can be washed and dressed and ready to embrace in an hour; an unscrubbed mind requires years to launder, and may never be worthy of embracing.

181. *Ignore* and *ignorance* are from the same root—to learn, you have to pay attention.

182. The ignorant are enemies of knowledge because the unknown is a source of fear, and men usually hate what they fear. Where there is much unknown, there is much fear. This explains why so many are unwilling to be instructed, or even to learn for themselves.

183. If an opinion, as it should be, is the result of careful and deliberate thought, then it is impossible to have an opinion on everything; there is not enough time spent thinking by any man to allow it.

184. The modern trend to assert that there is nothing unusual about anything—that everyone has certain feelings or goes through such a stage, or thinks so and so, or that X is not sur-

prising, or that every event or newly discovered fact should be taken casually — all this amounts simply to an excuse not to care. What we need today is more caring, and a renewed sense of awe. There are many neat and wonderful things happening or existing around us, and we should appreciate them with child-like wonder. The old, "Doesn't surprise me" bit is a confession of crass insensitivity or carelessness. When was the last time you were awed by a rain, or wind; or when were you last amazed at the power and usefulness of compressed air? Isn't it handy the way fruit grows pre-packaged in an edible skin or a peelable skin? Or do you "hmmph" when you see cumulus clouds building before your eyes? Did you ever examine a *snail* with close attention? Turn to man-made items. Do you take for granted such miracles as automobiles, hot and cold running water and *flush toilets*?

185. Flying very low is very dangerous. At three thousand feet, losing a hundred feet is called "losing a hundred feet"; at one hundred feet, losing a hundred feet is called "crashing."

186. The invitation of Matthew 11:28-30 so often goes unaccepted because man's ego is such that he is unwilling to submit himself, even to relieve the burdens he carries. He will try to pull his own load — his own burden of life — even though he does not know how. To submit to an instructor is an admission of inferiority in the instructor's field — and who, alas, will allow himself to admit inferiority to anyone in anything? See Glimmerings #179 and #182.

187. If the perpetrator of a crime, however small or uncostly, is allowed to continue unchecked and unpunished, his sense of morality will continue to decline below the level which has already permitted him to commit a small act of evil. His moral level or moral consciousness will soon be at a point where he will not think he is doing wrong when committing his original act; this will lead him to consider certain allied but worse crimes, and to engage in those acts which seem to follow his

previous ones. Thus, he who begins by visiting prostitutes will soon be seducing your daughter, and soon after, raping your wife. It is difficult for society to stand still either improving or declining. And, philosophy aside, there is much militant opposition to good.

188. Form your plans within your ability to execute them. Do not be always making plans you have no intention — or capacity — to carry out.

189. Curiosity, it is said, is a sign of intelligence. Yet we see many all around us with blank and uncaring looks: are so many excluded from the club of the knowing? I am afraid so. And how painful that it should be by their own choice. There is a major problem in contemporary society: so many people just do not care — about anything. They care not about their appearance, their morals, their intellectual capacities; they care not about other people's happiness, rights, or lives. Every man would please only himself, and that by immediate and complete gratification.

190. It is a fact greatly to be lamented that the body matures faster than the personality or the intellect. Could we be settled in our manners and attitudes by the time the body begins its sexual stirring, we would have very many happy teenage marriages. However, there would still remain the difficulty of losing one's singularity at so early an age. It is desirable, some say, to be independent during the teen and early twenties years, in order to explore freely — to meet a variety of characters and to see or take part in many different things, all of which would be hindered or prevented by the encumbrance of a constant second party of the opposite sex. Whether this is indeed true, or a valid reason, I do not know.

191. The worst that can happen to a man in a marriage, apart from spousal ridicule, disobedience, and infidelity, is intellectual horror and disgust, psychological torture, and emotional mu-

tilation. The worst that can happen to a man by remaining single is loneliness. However, the best that can happen to a man in a marriage, apart from spousal support, obedience, and loyalty, is intellectual satisfaction and companionship, psychological joy, and emotional sustenance; while the best that can happen to a man by remaining single is loneliness. Socrates, I think, said, "Whether you marry or stay single, you'll be sorry." Perhaps this is true. There are benefits and inconveniences in both states; there is freedom in being single, but there are freedoms in marriage as well. Marriage is not a solution but a change of state.

192. The modern teacher's Wishywashism — the refusal to take a positive stand, to pin things down, to give definite guidance, or to have set rules — has done as much to corrupt and dilute the minds of the young as all the other liberal idiocies put together. The student needs guidance and instruction. He cannot choose for himself the things he has yet to learn until he is taught how to discriminate. When a thirsty child comes to us for water we do not toss him into the middle of a lake and exclaim, "Drink anything you want!" We instead dip him a cup of the freshest, clearest water and help him sip it. That way, in future years, he will be able to find and drink the best water, instead of diving face first into the mud of the lake as his Wishywashist teacher seemed to indicate.

193. It is tearfully unfortunate that so many geniuses are freens. They who most deserve the happy companionship of a beautiful girl are most repulsive to beauty. And so the genius is condemned to solitude and loneliness, and the price of intellectual superiority is emotional distress. The same is true of highly intelligent girls also; many of them are similarly weird, awkward, unusually proportioned, and possessed of odd personalities. Perhaps the saddest part is that freens are not attractive to each other; for even freens have eyes and taste.

194. I should qualify Glimmering #193 a little. By "a beautiful girl" I do not mean the facially super cute girl who has learned

to manipulate people with her looks, and has neglected the development of every other virtue and faculty, since she can get anything she wants with a smile. No, such females do not generate "happy companionship"; they tend to be aggressive, selfish, ignorant, insulting, bossy, capricious, and obstinate. I am speaking of the normal, healthy young lady of average attractiveness and above average intelligence, et cetera.

195. The brightest are not those who nod their heads, but those who ask questions.

196. Sometimes giving attention to a problem worsens it instead of ameliorating or curing it. But the effort and intention to bring about good are to be commended. There are so many who simply sit and do nothing that action is almost a virtue in itself.

197. Happiness is best achieved by little blessings properly considered and little possessions properly enjoyed. If you have not the sensitivity to appreciate small things, then great miracles and great riches will not make you happy. If you do have the sensitivity, you do not need the miracles or riches.

198. I have tried to get three women to read the *Ramblers*; not a one has read any.

199. There is a time appointed for each man to die, after which his deeds will be forgotten or distorted and his thoughts lost. Every one should therefore take care to write down some words of encouragement, some lessons from experience, some precepts of morality, some admonitions to piety, and some statements of truth. The written word preserves the essence of thoughts and deeds for the use and aid of future generations, and allows those who are willing to read to begin life at a point above that at which their predecessors were compelled to start. What greater comfort can there be to an old man anxious to enter the arms of the Lord, than to know he has said and taught all he can, and has preserved his knowledge for his children and

grandchildren? He alone can lie back comfortably and proclaim, "I have written, and now I can die."

200. Something valuable should be imagined and written down every day, in a form as concise as possible. Certainly if we put our minds to it we can invent some maxim of use, or better, open our minds to the Lord to receive one. After all, time and health and eyesight will not be taken for granted.

201. The ability to see beneath rust to a valuable core may be useful in human relations also. Rust can be burnished off.

202. If you surround yourself with the cultural trappings of only one age, you will share its follies, fads, and discontents as well. Be culturally eclectic, and choose upon the principles of taste and merit rather than age or popularity.

203. We are taught by a simple law of physics that he who quickly leaps into a scheme and flies away will undoubtedly bounce off the first wall of opposition or difficulty, since his ability to gain momentum so rapidly betrays a great lack of weight. Conversely, the man who raises his scheme slowly and with careful deliberation, and who accelerates it gradually will be almost impossible to stop, or even delay. The weightiness of his scheme will carry it unalterably forward, wreaking horrible violence and destruction upon any opposition, and requiring supernatural energies to halt.

204. Whether it is wrong, an insult to this age, or a shortchanging of my contemporaries, I do not know; but I consider my duty to posterity more important than my duty to my fellow coevals.

205. Many people seem to arrange their beliefs or understandings in circles, and to race around in a "thinking car" which never reaches new territory, but only reinforces the few ideas already present, by racing around in circles. These persons are

unwilling to admit new ideas or possibilities which would extend their track and boundaries, because they are afraid to break the old familiar circle. Neither are they willing for the same reason to pave new roads of their own through enquiry or experiment.

206. Life is happiest when varied by the uncertainty of risk and the involvement of challenge.

207. A bolt, tightened beyond its torque capacity into a tapped hole, will be permanently deformed and then twisted off. That not only destroys the bolt but creates a difficulty in removing the stub left overtightened in the hole. The same law applies to people. A man strained beyond his capacities in a given emotional, physical, or intellectual situation will not only break, ruining himself, but will cause great damage in the area around him. He will make a decision leading the company into trouble; he will say or do things to others which may not be capable of remedy. Yet the course of life and promotion and success is to see how much torque every man can take.

208. The progress of knowledge is greatly hindered today because most people would rather simply get their own point or opinion across than discover the truth in a matter. Few are willing to ask questions to supply ignorance; fewer are willing to hear arguments for other opinions. When a man realizes that his own beliefs may be in error, and that his own opinions may be wrongly based, and that the words of a fool may sometime instruct him, then his ego is in its proper place.

209. Much of the worry, care, and argument of this life can be avoided entirely just by knowing the difference between what is important and what is not important. Only a few things matter, and their significance is such that no one can afford to expend time away from them upon idle and empty apprehensions.

210. A happy marriage requires mutual loyalty and trust and

deference, and a satisfactory hierarchy of command.

211. People do not corrupt themselves as fast as they are corrupted by others.

212. How disappointed I am at the corrupt morality and the syrupy liberalism everywhere preached at the university. And the textbooks, which pretend to guide the students to truth, are the worst of all.

213. What a miracle that even a man of modest means can, by owning a record player, invite troubadours and chamber orchestras into his room to play and sing for him every morning. What wealth would have been required for such a thing in the past.

214. There are two classes of intellects and of general workers: plodders and blazers. Those who blaze are immensely spectacular in rapid but limited accomplishment, and they are at any rate soon extinguished. Who is left to do the work? The plodders. It may be a little like the hare and the tortoise. Who is the real hero — the professor who supplies a flash of insight to unite hundreds of pages of notes into a unifying theory, or the researcher who supplies the sweat and eyestrain to accumulate the notes? Blazers are more glorious, but plodders are probably of equal value in contributing to the necessities of earthly life. The wind is indeed an elegant and mysterious force which spins the globe, but its task would be impossible if someone did not grease the bearings of the axis.
 And finally, we regard the saying, "Boys make plans and girls carry them out," and conclude that each sex is indispensable to the other.

215. Too much time is devoted to equalizing areas which should have hierarchies, and to creating hierarchies in areas which should have equality.

216. What does any man do for a living but try?

217. Give a ten word plot summary of the Old Testament. Be as specific as possible.

218. If life actually went exactly according to our plans, I don't think the tone or volume of our screams would really be much different.

219. If my razor should prove ineffective against their twisted bodies, calloused with evil, then perhaps my sledge hammer will attract their attention.

220. What is more delicious than the smell of burning wood on a cool and moist evening?

221. The culpability for some of our mistakes will I think be somewhat mitigated when, at the Last Judgment, we plead that what we did was based on a decision which seemed to be the right one at the time. How many follies have we committed which seemed perfectly reasonable and right when we decided to indulge, and yet which now give us pain to think upon, because we cannot comprehend the existence of such stupidity in our own heads!

222. Not enough is made of man's duties today. We each should have a strong sense of duty, not only because it is right and necessary to obey our duties, but because a sense of duty contributes in a large way to personal stability and happiness. The rootless, dutiless person will always be discontent.

223. It is man's duty to accept miscarriages with equanimity. The strength and character of a man can be read in the way he behaves after a defeat. Victories should be cherished with modesty, because no one can know how much he was responsible for it and how much was contributed by the Lord, by others, or by circumstance. For what character has he who is willing to

gloat in victory but who would mope in defeat?

224. Another way to state Glimmering #209: Half the misery of life can be avoided by knowing what is not important and forgetting about it.

225. It is a hard lesson for the virtuous to accept, but most men do not want deliverance from evil; they want only safety and security in which to perform it.

226. If any of us who are conscious of sin should for a moment consider the limitless quantity of mercy extended to each one of us by the Lord during the course of a single day, how could we fail to burn with forgiveness for the petty wrongs worked against us?

227. The dead heads in overactive bodies will be the ruin of us all.

228. Take nothing for granted, and realize that all hopes may fail—then you will never be disappointed. Plan for every contingency; have alternatives for your alternative plans; know what you will do if the worst occurs.

229. Beware of him who praises your ideas yet fails to act upon them; do not let him be the judge of your perfections or the critic of your flaws.

230. How sad it is for a man to be so insecure as to be hungry for praise, and so egotistical as to believe it.

231. To be last is to get there; to quit is not to start.

232. It's always a particular irony to spell the word *intelligently* wrong.

233. Genius is a product of ability, good taste, and hard work.

234. The key to the quality of life, the prerequisite for happiness, is emotional, physical, intellectual, and spiritual assurance. It is all basically a matter of security.

235. Intellectual security, as it relates to the quality of life, is advanced by education and aesthetic training. Aesthetics consists of environment (air, water, plants), safety (of persons and property), and decoration.

236. Many men are too concerned with seeking personal solutions instead of laboring to advance the quality of life and the civilization of mankind. This is achieved by seeking solutions to the problems of others, or to shared problems.

237. No more perverse, stubborn, or erroneous decisions are made than when some heated or disgruntled thinker suddenly decides to make up his own mind, in opposition to the advice of friends and counselors. Thinking for oneself is a condition to be arrived at slowly, through care and experience. He who would suddenly decide for himself has no tools to work with; and when his folly is remarked, can fall back only upon stubbornness.

238. Motto of the Modern High School: Don't teach them anything they don't already know; it will only confuse them.

239. Reading assignments in good texts and literary works should be kept short to allow time for contemplation and re-reading.

240. There is an extreme weakness of aesthetic perception in college freshmen (18 year olds). They have little sense of beauty, elegance, or refinement. What have they been learning? And worse than this aesthetic lack is the emptiness of spiritual feeling I find in them. They have no religious emotion, no spiritual direction. They have no valuable sensitivities — only intemper-

ate and unreasonable emotional reactions. Instead of their feelings working in conjunction with reason, reason is displaced and gut feeling takes over—working against the intellect. And to speak of verbal abilities is not to speak of them. Was I that savage and uncouth at eighteen?

241. A relatively few authors and books have been selected by literary scholars and critics, with the result that these works are interpreted to death. Many good books are ignored, while the popular ones are subjected to every kind of bizarre twisting imaginable, to allow some PhD a "new" interpretation or insight. Critics should put out editions and explications of less well known but deserving works.

242. I wonder if that talk isn't just hot air under a blanket, imitating substance.

243. The words "family member" form a child's first title of responsibility, and require of him his first duties.

244. Every piece of good advice, every maxim or quintessential summary of some aspect of life, was paid for very dearly by someone, who later swallowed his pride and generously offered to teach others from the textbook of his own mistakes.

245. Reading and travel are the two primary sources of new ideas and further education. Discussion is too often an empty contest or exchange of fashionable lies.

246. Life should be led the easiest way possible within the boundaries of duty, service, and virtue; and without ignoring justice or decency.

247. He who succumbs to flattery is greatly to be pitied. He sells himself for the price of a few words idly spoken; which words he knows not to be true, and which the flatterer believes not to be true. These are words spoken in counterfeit and accepted in

hypocrisy, yet exchanged, rated, and rewarded as if genuine.

248. Take what was intended for evil and draw out of it some service to the Lord. Change wicked intentions into good results.

249. Spreading kindness is important; spreading justice is more important. Being friendly is important; being virtuous is more important.

250. How strange an organ is the human ego. It is quite weak, yet is always blustering around in bully fashion; it is extremely tender and easily damaged, yet not even repeatedly severe blows are fatal; it is an enormous organ, yet is very easily inflated further, and easily inflated further still—with not the least danger of breaking, unless pricked. This organ is constantly massaged and soothed by its owner, yet is frequently found to be sore and irritable; it is fed constantly by the owner and his friends, yet is still always hungry. It is jealous of territory it cannot keep and has no right to. Nay, it is jealous of territory it has not seen, or even has merely imagined.

251. There is no feeling like that of knowing what you're doing—even when you don't.

252. How sad it is to pat a tree uprooted by the wind. When you pat the trunk of a growing tree, it is solid and sturdy. But when the trunk changes from vertical to horizontal, the feeling is altogether different. What a sense of helpless defeat to pace out the length of a canceled tree.

253. We are fighting a war in our earthly existence. In any war, some battles will be lost. We must then retrench, regroup, and attack—or defend—again. And we must remember that there will be casualties even in the battles we win.

254. The best way to guarantee success in your daily endeavors and to limit frustration in your life is simply to have an alternate

plan. If you plan to visit x store and buy y item, be prepared in case x store is closed or y item is sold out. Never expect everything to go perfectly. Don't allow a single small defeat (or two or three) to "ruin" your day. Have you ever heard a general say, "We were going to attack the enemy today, but we couldn't get one of our tanks started, so we quit"? Naturally I don't expect you to bring a TV to church in case your bride doesn't show up on your wedding day—some things are important in themselves as far as success goes. But generally too much emphasis is placed on relatively insignificant details of daily life, which, if you plan around when they fall through, will not bother you half as much as they do now. Make contingency plans: don't let too much ride on the outcome of any uncertain event. You will be not only happier but more successful, too.

255. Our duty is not to excel each other, but to serve God to the extent of our granted capacity.

256. Patience is a virtue we all should learn.—Yes, well, how long will it take? I haven't got much time.

257. Sleep not without reading—or writing—a pious thought. Do not worry if your thought is "just common sense" or is "obvious": it is by obvious maxims and common sense timely remembered that we learn to practice virtue.

258. Most people are too busy being somebody else's problem to find their own solutions. All complain; few mitigate.

259. I'm torn between writing severe satires and being a kind and generous person. I don't know why. I want to be a positive force making others happy, but I'm by nature a very negative person. Then too, I see evil everywhere in the world, crying out to be criticized and chopped down to size.

260. Perseverance will accomplish almost anything in the other endeavors of man; but, when it comes to people, there is noth-

ing so intractable as the human psyche. The uncertainty of success in human relations is so considerable that I become discouraged and quit after only a few failures. It is surprising how many people do not want to be helped.

261. A very valuable quality now lost by the twentieth century is respect for disagreement. Those who do not share our views can teach us a lot more than those who agree with us—there is a limited amount to be learned by looking in the mirror. When we meet someone of a different opinion, we are forced to examine, shape up, and codify our reasons to make sure they can stand up to the opposition; we can get an understanding of the opponent's point of view and his reasons; we can gain by reexamining our ideas, which may need altering, discarding, or reinforcing. No one has an opinion on everything. If we can hear two sides adequately presented, we can choose our stand; if only one side is presented, we have not enough information to make a choice.

262. Even obvious things, perhaps obvious things especially, need to be stated. There is much truth in obviousness; many truths exist in the world plainly and frankly, but since we cannot hold them all in our minds at once, it is a good thing to be reminded of them frequently.

263. Always "remind" people of things—though they have never heard any of them before. That is the only way to get around Pride the doorman.

264. Whenever we begin an undertaking of uncertain outcome, we usually—if not always—assume that it would be best to succeed. That is often a mistake. Pray not for success, but for God's will; otherwise, you may be praying for madness or evil.

265. It is not enough to know what you believe; you must know why.

266. To be a perfectionist regarding your own activities is fine — all that will do is drive you insane or create chronic depression because of your shortcomings. But to require perfection in others is not only total madness from the outset, but it discovers a latent masochism. He who seeks perfection from his associates, employees, or students is destined to writhe on a spit, roasted by frustration and disappointment; he will crack his joints on a rack, tortured by worry and fear; he will climb the steps of hope only to crash through the trap of broken promise, with a rope, braided from laziness and inconstancy, tightening around his neck.

267. All great art is the product of extraordinary discipline manipulating artistic conventions in such a way as both to embody and to excel them. It is the challenge of working within a form or style or genre which produces the effort needed to achieve greatness. The moment you protest that artistic conventions shackle your creativity is the moment you resign your chance to be great.

268. Humility is so rare today that anyone possessing it would be inclined to brag. Wouldn't it inflate your ego to know you were so rare as to be humble?

269. However much we may enjoy variety and newness in life, or agree about the necessity for flexibility and progress, half the happiness of mankind is derived from the assurance of sameness in our environment and in our associates. Think of the convenience of unchanging timetables — but more, think of the implications and the reasons behind such virtues as fidelity (unchangingly loyal), constancy, trust, reliability. A familiar spot is loved for its sameness. Sameness gives security. We form habits because they are easy by their regularity — their sameness. How we fear and dislike unreliable people: it is by far better to know for sure whether you are safe or will be betrayed than to be ever in uncertainty. What anxieties can unpredictable people cause.

270. You have no obligation to grant what another has no right to ask.

271. An exact knowledge of grammar is the key to intellectual freedom. If your words make no sense, your thoughts won't either.

272. It is an irony that the best students have the most anxiety about doing well.

273. Hierarchies of command are necessary for happiness and security as well as for efficiency.

274. Nothing contrary to the Word of God should be offered to the Lord; to do so would be to offer strange fire. He who genuinely seeks to serve God will seek out by careful examination of the Bible the acceptable ways of service and the proper values involved. Every good thing in the world can be perverted or counterfeited or both; be careful of those who would seem to serve God but who produce bad results or achieve their ends by immoral or questionable means. Know them by their fruits—are the fruits grown according to God's instructions, or were they stolen from another's orchard? Test the spirits; test your own plans and intentions.

275. "Wine, women, and song," three good things, can each be perverted either in themselves or by improper use. Wine is perverted in itself when it is badly or cheaply made, when it is not properly stored, or when it otherwise becomes ruined; it is perverted by improper use when Herbert's rule against the third glass is broken. Women are perverted in themselves when they are selfish, petty, hateful, loose, aggressive, or "liberated"; they are perverted by improper use when abused sexually or psychologically, or when cast in unfeminine situations. Song is perverted in itself when it shows no talent, "harmony," value, taste, or decency; it is perverted by improper use when employed to manipulate emotions against the hearer's will, or when it is in-

terrupted by conversation (divertimentos notwithstanding).

276. The household economy in our century is complex and difficult to run: it requires a full-time employee.

277. Flee Pride—and never stop to congratulate yourself for reaching a safe distance.

278. But then, the stars are brightest on the coldest nights.

279. People realize now that in dealing with salesmen there is no such thing as *free*; these people are also beginning to realize that the same is true with government. There are no free services or programs—someone pays for each and every one of them, either through taxes or through inflation. And with the gross inefficiency of government, an enormous amount of taxes or inflation is needed to pay for even the smallest of services. The government has no money of its own; all it does or can do is process the money of others or counterfeit (i.e., print) the money of others. Of these two things—stealing your money in taxes and diluting with counterfeit money—the latter is the worse crime, because it interferes with economic planning and lowers the standard of living in a behind-hand way.

280. If you pull out all the stops, you might go down the drain.

281. Life is not really the series of uninterrupted crises we make it out to be.

282. When was the last time you heard someone admit that he didn't have enough information to form a conclusion? Almost all people are ready—too ready—to draw conclusions from the few imperfect and incomplete facts in their possession. Rare is the man who will take the trouble to seek more information before forming an opinion.

283. The entire filthy world is hosed off by a succession of tiny

raindrops. Continue in your actions, however small, and they will not fail to have an effect.

284. It is not the number but the choice of books that is the key to education—and to wisdom. What an immense amount of time is wasted grinding away at garbage books! And what injuries they do to our souls.

285. I will be a soul doctor, and a doctor of the intellect; my prescriptions are found in books and are taken in through the eyes.

286. Rain makes a calm, gentle, exhaling, rushing sound when it falls through the sky; when it hits, it makes another sound which varies according to the landing place. It might thud to earth, plop or snap into water, dink on metal, slap on a plant leaf. Wherever it spreads its essence, it is welcomed and blessed.

287. How a hot desire to write and a frozen invention do wrestle one another.

288. We spendthriftily seek protection from every excess of nature—sun, heat, cold, snow, wind—but expensively indulge unnatural excesses to our much greater harm. We curse the excesses of nature and complain about them unceasingly; we praise the excesses of unnature and seek to involve others in them.

289. His words had all the subtlety of bear breath.

290. We should combine *dulce et utile*, sweetness and light, pleasure and instruction, beauty and utility, art and practicality, in everything—not just in literature. As a gift, offer a teapot filled with tea bags; this brings immediate pleasure for the senses, and provides a lasting useful gift. Automobiles, when assembled carefully, combine *dulce et utile* nicely.

291. These writers whom we admire and value as "classics" all had one trait in common: they believed in, stated, and argued conclusions. They had definite, usually quite exact opinions. Pick up Aristotle or Horace. Note how specific they are. We find them excellent partly because they are not trivial or evasive the way many current writers are. Read Samuel Johnson. He was certainly sometimes wrong—even bigotedly wrong—but you always had an opinion of him: he made positive assertions, the majority of which have been now filed among the eternal verities perceptible by man.

If you want your work to live and to be useful, be positive, definite, and specific—and forget about the critics who will call you dogmatic, superficial, or simplistic. Assertions, even if wrong, stir the imagination of the reader; vague wishy washiness, even if indisputable, does nothing but compel one to sleep. If you are a careful thinker, it is better to risk making a wrong assertion or a bad judgment than to be correctly and securely namby pamby.

292. The deliciousness of rain—yes, rain sometimes looks delicious—rain gently falling into random puddles with uneven, ragged edges—this rain forms order out of chaos by creating an infinite series of successive perfect circles wherever a single drop lands. We note a good mustiness in the air. Who could think that even dirt could smell so satisfying? Listen to the steady drip from the roof onto the plants; see the free-running streams and rivulets, emerging from places unknown and wandering to places unsuspected. Rain turned into miniature rivers rewrites geography. New waterways appear—but more, these waterways disclose the existence of hills and slopes and valleys we knew not of, nor dreamed of. Who thought that was down hill? How low lies the floor of that new lakelet! What a hump, what an Ararat, rises there! Many small lakes fill up; all are beautifully bordered and most are clear—until we splash gleefully through them destroying the lakeside resorts and not doing the smoothness of the bottom any good, either. What equals the plop of water?

293. There are four kinds of economic demand. 1). Ordinary demand. Supply rises to meet it, and price balance is kept. 2). Extraordinary demand. In the case of a sudden fad, when supply cannot rise fast enough, when the supply is limited in absolute amount and demand exceeds it or when the supply was planned wrong—i.e., unforeseen demand. Example of these last two together would be a fixed number of new homes in a tract (absolute amount), and the quantity of some wines bottled a few years ago now popular, resulting in "wrong" planned supply, which cannot now be increased. 3). Unique demand. Custom made items for which only one buyer exists. 4). Transferred Demand. When the price of one product rises excessively, demand for substitute products will increase, and this may increase the price of the substitute products. When coffee rises to $3 a pound, tea may go up also. Supply is similar. Briefly 1). ordinary supply 2). extraordinary supply—Demand was not strong enough or too man made. 3). Unique supply—a work of art, etc. Only one item for several would-be buyers.

294. If I could add together every set of five minutes that I've frittered away, I'd have time to write an epic.

295. Much of life seems to be a training course for endurance.

296. New things, old things, new ways, old ways. I find four ways of combining these concepts according to the manner they may be used or viewed. To use or view
    1. A new thing in a new way is called Invention.
    2. An old thing in an old way is called Tradition.
    3. A new thing in an old way is called Classification.
    4. An old thing in a new way is called Application.

297. It is our nature to complain, our destiny to praise. Should we not seek our destiny?

298. Just because we do not understand a thing does not make it

wrong or needless. What a prideful sense of one's understanding it is to condemn what is not comprehended.

299. We have no great or timeless works of literary theory in the twentieth century because they are not permitted. Take a look at Aristotle, Horace, Boileau, Sidney—it is the straightforward simplicity comprehending great ideas which makes the works great; yet today there is a vicious feeling against simplicity, exactness, definiteness. Somehow truth must be always incomprehensibly complex and dragged out over a hundred pages of limping prose filled with qualifiers and uncertainties. Wanted are paradoxes, endless intricacies, obscurities, difficulties, manifold multiplicities. Wanting is affirmation—the risk of an assertion—truth itself. Truth is indeed complex; but boiled down, it has a simple foundation. A man may be differentiated from a woman without invoking DNA helixes, chromosomes, hormones, or autopsies. Let us first hear the main clause; we will attend to the subordinate clauses and modifiers later. The purpose of a treatise on art or of any statement of philosophy which sets out to call attention to some systematic principle is not to exhaust all the intricacies and nuances of a subject and then to tire out all its implications and repercussions. No; rather, it is to set a foundation on which to build—to scrape the moss off the ground and find the rock which will hold the rest up.

300. The key to poetry is association.

301. The stream seems widest as you stand on the shore ready to cross; not so wide from midstream; hardly half what you imagined as you stand on the far shore looking back.

302. Oh no, you have it backwards. A man's life—his soul—does not exist for the sake of his intestines. Who measures success by counting dollars—or sausages—succeeds not at all; success lies in moral victory. But, you say, one cannot buy food with moral victory. Indeed not, but if life becomes insupportable on that basis, why 'tis better to give it over and join the

Lord. The further stuffing of your guts will please the worms awhile longer, but perhaps improve not man nor serve God.

303.

1. Trust God
2. Do Your Duty
3. Persevere

and do not worry about the future or the outcome of any endeavor. If you succeed, you will have done so honestly; if you fail, your effort will be not only praised but rewarded.

304. In writing his critical papers, the graduate student desires to break new ground, to unearth something previously hidden from all others; yet he usually has neither the strength nor the tools to do it. So, most of the time, in spite of his efforts, he finds himself merely flopping and raking the surface dung of previous critics who have wandered by that way.

305. The two greatest dangers to any undertaking—whether a geographical exploration, a research project, or a business proposition—are hurry and fragmentation. The proper time must be allowed for each step, and the facilities and resources must remain concentrated. Not allowing yourself adequate time or diluting your materials, your concentration, or yourself will inevitably lead to failure. Time is easier to reckon with—you can learn to pace yourself. But the temptation to fragmentation will always be a great one. Do not spread yourself too thin. Do not attempt too many things at once, give your attention to too many areas, or go in too many directions. Fifty men, each with a club, will be unable to break through into the castle of the unknown. But put them together on a single ramrod and they will soon have the door down.

The second two great enemies of an undertaking are inadequate foresight and inadequate provision. Chances are your undertaking will not be as easy as sitting in the shade reading an adventure story. Plan for the unplanned: this is old advice, yet it is too often ignored. What are your contingency plans?

You must form an alternate plan for every part of your journey, and then a substitute for that alternate. It is frequently better and easier to have an alternative mode than to attempt to beef up your main plan so much that it must succeed. When anyone asks of you, "What if you fail?" it may be heroic to answer, "I have planned so that I cannot fail," but it is unrealistic.

Foresight is necessary in the matter of provisions also. Whether your supplies are to be foodstuffs, books, or capital reserves, you must do your best to have enough for the completion of the project. To have a ninety-nine foot rope at the bottom of a one hundred foot cliff is little different from having no rope at all. How sad to have eleven months' rent when twelve months were needed. When three bailing cans would have seen your ship through the storm and into port, it were a sad matter for your final thoughts to have had only two. I would rather have a sore shoulder and a gallon canteen full of water as I reached the Colorado River than to lie in the middle of the Mojave Desert wishing for a single drop.

306. Marginally interested in education, they sometimes come, half in disbelief, to see if you are still going on about the same book.

307. Of all things which seduce men from the path of reason, a major one is the internal combustion engine, whatever form it may be found in—automobile, motorcycle, lawn mower, snowmobile, airplane, motorboat, tree saw. From which we conclude that a very great danger to happiness is the unreasonable pursuit and use of power.

308. Ambition is almost always promoted under another name; because although ambition in moderation—the desire to better oneself through industriousness—is praised, the vices of ambitious excesses, overreaching and *hubris*, are among the worst of crimes. Excess ambition is sometimes considered antisocial and selfish, or even verging on blasphemy.

309. What terror, hatred, and emotional distress do modern writers work upon us in the name of "new" truth.

310. You know the honeymoon is over when, after you tell your wife you're cold, she reaches over and turns up the electric blanket.

311 He was urging Atropos to pick up her scissors.

312. Three things not very much in demand are virtue, stainless steel light bulbs, and Dr. Kluts' *How to Feel Ten Percent Better in Only a Year*.

313. A maxim from one of my students: You become what you read.

314. Happiness is attendant upon values. Morality is necessary for happiness. Pursuing pleasure is a specious detour which leads ultimately away from happiness.

315. When it is abused or unwanted, reason will not stay long.

316. We, like moths, must navigate the path of our lives by a fixed point of light. But too often the candle flame of worldliness attracts us from the true moonlight of the Lord, and we fly away into the flame and burn forever.

317. A man marries in order not to need an electric blanket or a television set; to marry and still to need an electric blanket and a television set is indeed a disappointment.

318. It was one of those well-known books which we have all read and hated.

319. He couldn't teach a possum to play dead, but he had written a book and so was granted tenure. How'd he do it? He bored the possum to death with a lecture.

320. The purpose of human existence is twofold: first, to serve and to please God; and second, to prepare ourselves and each other for our eternal estate in Heaven. Our duty in life then is also twofold: first to learn, and by learning to gain a knowledge of the right and just, to gain the wisdom to do good, and to gain the understanding to fulfill our social obligations as moral and productive citizens contributing to the lives of those around us; second, to teach others what we have learned. We must teach ourselves to think and to avoid delusion.

321. "Better late than broken." A useful old proverb, this can be called to mind by a driver about to pass a car in dangerous traffic, a bicyclist in a hurry to get to class, a server with an armful of food and drink for table 3, etc.

322. Some experiences in life are like the smell of cut grass: pleasant in its own way, but not a smell to have always in one's nostrils.

323. She was the perfection of mortal beauty—so beautiful was she, in fact, that it would distress you to look at her.

324. Snobbery is merely class egotism.

325. A careful reading, rereading, and thoughtful mastery of a certain number of well-chosen books (primarily the classics) would be of infinitely more value in the education of a student than the current reading practice, where the student is required to read hurriedly and cursorily through an enormous number of books, many of questionable or no value. For a good book to educate properly, the student needs time to interact with its ideas; he must be able to pause and *think* frequently. Too many classics are now jammed together into too short a period of time for reading them. This is made worse by the added piles of junk commentaries assigned as extra reading. Leave the student alone with a good book for awhile, let him think about it, and

you will be able to dispense with 90% of the criticism you now require.

Textbooks worsen the bad situation by diluting and discussing (boringly) the ideas which were better read in the original works. Reading a predigested pulpation of Aristotle or Newton is no way to train your mind.

326. In the Old West justice didn't grind slowly; it often traveled at the speed of a bullet, or at approximately the same speed crime traveled.

327. The more you read in a confined period of time, the less you learn. Learning requires mastery; mastery requires slow reading. Simply turning over a lot of pages is of limited value. Further, if you read for enjoyment as well as for enlightenment, what enjoyment is gained from rushing? You wouldn't pretend to sight-see at 100 miles per hour; you don't gulp down steak and lobster; you don't glance at great paintings; you don't give a flower a single sniff. If quantity does not make friends with time, the sweetness is untasted and the light is missed by a blink.

328. A large part of knowledge, explanation, and understanding is the result of and relies on—is inseparable from—association. We use simile and analogy for explanation as well as beauty. The best poetry is that which has the best associations—similes, metaphors. The mind is largely a combining device which can miraculously extract points of similarity or difference, or mesh ideas in wonderful ways.

329. That poor hack writer's Alexandrine lines result from too much scraping in his mental mines.

330. They enlarge their ignorance by compounding it with false distillations and wrong learning.

331. In Hell the fire is black.

332. This new position of authority didn't go to his head as you might suspect—instead it went straight to his ego.

333. Is the refrigeration cycle the greatest invention since 1800?

334. There are no isolated actions just as there are no isolated thoughts.

335. Falsehood is never opposed half so vigorously as is truth.

336. The happiness of society is based on order; the order, on law.

337. One of the bases of a harmonious and lasting marriage is mutual solicitation of the other's happiness. When selfishness in either partner arises, the marriage is in danger. If each seeks to please the other, a strong and permanent union will result.

338. I wasn't sure whether to blame him for being drunk or excuse him for being crazy.

339. To say he's the best professor in the world is not to say much, for professors are a pretty pitiful lot.

340. Men find hateful or lovable, bad or good, what they desire to find hateful, lovable, bad, or good; their prejudices color their perceptions. Or to quote the old proverb, He who stuffs excrement up his nose will find the smell of everything afterwards peculiar.

341. Professor Tweedle's book is an assemblage of banalities interspersed by platitudes and trite remarks.

342. Whatever setbacks you may receive, however blunted your edge may become, keep moving. No matter how much you need to thrash, dodge, struggle, or slow, always advance. Let

nothing stall you and you will be invincible.

343. To be sure, this is the best half-baked book I've ever read.

344. Every so often a list is gathered of all the mistaken readings, clumsy paraphrasing, drunken symbolizing, invented profundities, pedantic inutilities, and general foolishness, wrongheadedness and buffooning that has been written about a poor, defenseless literary work, whose dead author, alas, cannot now laugh or call names. Such a list is called a critical bibliography and is more respected by the Ph.D.'s than is the literary work itself.

345. Life was integrated in the Renaissance. Art, architecture, science, poetry, philosophy, and religion were all part of each man.

346. Man is willing to run his guts out for the proud feeling of success, but is often little enough moved by charity or compassion.

347. The average doctor is no more competent than the average auto mechanic. Both frequently misdiagnose a condition because of ignorance, laziness, or carelessness. Each has his prejudices or favorite treatments. Both occasionally treat only symptoms (a procedure much easier than critical thinking and analysis), and try first one remedy and then another (whether a new part or a new pill), hoping that the latest will finally fix the problem. Whether successful or not, the bill is the same.

348. Birth into existence is not enough, but fulfillment. Don't vegetate, act. Push your inventions—nay, your very life—to fulfillment. Do not linger in the idle realm of being. See Marcus Aurelius VI. 1.

349. Throwing rocks in an attempt to damage the ocean causes a splash and a sore arm.

350. "They have not wits and are therefore not dangerous."
   "Why Sir, we may be overtaken by witless amoebic dysentery."

351. The aggressive too often act without reflection. They see all restraints as evil; yet reason is a restraint. To reject reason is to howl at the moon by night.

352. They never learn or teach anything because they never pin anything down. They are so careful with qualifiers and modifiers that the main clause is lost or buried or never expressed.

353. "We speak in the present tense because the past is nothing to us."
   "But why were we not told that this would happen?"

354. Folly is a vice arising from an enlarged ego and a diminished judgment.

355. There is consolation in eternity for every Christian, and even the life of him who has never done anything right has still been valuable in preparing for the world to come by teaching through mistake and distress.

356. A. B. Diel—his words were sweet, but his voice was that of the devil.

357. How sad it is to leaf through a used copy of some priceless volume and to find the editor's introduction underlined and marked, but not a mark on the text itself.

358. If you come upon a good book, do not be content with just reading it; make it a part of yourself by a close study and frequent rereading.

359. Since I plan to present nothing but the most gustatory ex-

cellences—a model of true taste—the reader may unconcernedly lap up the entire conglomeration of ingredients, without inquiring too nicely where they are from or what they will do to him.

360. I have stolen nothing, though I may have rented a point or two here and there.

361. The back shelves are filled first.

362. One reason so many people are dissatisfied with life is that they are always wanting new blessings, instead of being content with the continuation of old ones. How soon is a great blessing taken for granted and forgotten!

363. The food we eat is compounded of two essences, of nutrients and waste. Our bodies process this material and recover the good—the highest is kept while the useless is flushed down the sewer. So should it be with our intellectual processes. We must examine incoming information and ideas, separate the good from the bad, and keep the true and noble while discarding the false and evil. Unfortunately, in modern society there are many who reject the good and who keep and multiply the bad. No one will eat excrement, but many will read it.

364. My anger is always raised by those pedants who after hearing or reading or even writing any generalization, must remark, "Of course it isn't as simple as that," which is a statement applicable to every generalization ever uttered, and so obvious that it insults the hearer. What these types cannot see is that we are trying to *understand* at large, not to define the subtleties and complexities of life in a sentence or two. We need generalizations to open vistas, to establish patterns, orders, rules, groups. Of *course* we know "it isn't as simple as that." As complex as life is, many would make it more complex in order to repeat previous knowledge in different, harder-to-understand language (this is called a "nuance"), or to allow them to sit back in awe

and smack their lips, assured that while they are incapable of solving any problem, so must every man else be who would avoid simplistic answers to complex problems.

But much worse than the disgusting patronization of those who would remind us that a generalization is not perfectly accurate in every adducible instance is the modernist unwillingness to allow any generalization at all. Everything must be restricted, reduced, qualified, specific, narrow. Such an attitude prevents the great books of theory of every kind from being written, while men of large and small capacity merely pick at details, some significant, some not.

"A tragedy is an imitation of an action" (Aristotle). Well, of course it isn't as simple as that, and you haven't said what kind of tragedy, which action, whose imitation. . . .

The great foundation works of art and science from Aristotle at least through the 18th century are all books of comprehensive generalization. Ask a Renaissance humanist what he sees, and he might say, "A forest showing the order and beauty of God's creation, and proving by its composition the overall harmony of flux and diversity." A modernist would say, "I see a brown pine needle fifteen centimeters in length and pointed on one end."

365. "I haven't read the poem itself, but I have read professor Bribble's famous book on it."

366. Don't spend so much time using up the clock. Do something of lasting value every day. The weak and thinning topsoil of civilization needs your help.

367. Even if your talent is only moderate—nay, though it be small indeed—it cannot help but pass by the wretched grovelings of a careless and evil pen now revered as wondrous art. And perhaps some line may ring true and inspire a future heaven-sent artist to dash boldly forth and rekindle in the world through art the artless love of God.

368. A prolonged pressure will bend, distort, or break almost

anything it is applied to. Beware then of the accuracy and quality of truths or statements derived from pressurized environments.

369. I have little patience with unbelievers. The door to life is standing open and in full view, but they won't accept the invitation to enter because one must stoop to go through. These unbelievers want to keep their noses in the air at all costs (lest their egos fall off) and therefore wander around seeking snooty substitutes for the spiritual fresh air which blows through the door.

370. It was as welcome a sight as a pile of dry wood termite poop.

371. Present yourself every day with an intellectual problem so that your mind may be taught to grapple, to think, to solve.

372. Who said, "It is not enough to speak, but to speak true?"

373. It is not merely the discoverers but the organizers of knowledge to whom we are indebted for civilization and wisdom. Systematizers are often scorned, but it is they who are our first and best teachers. One must encompass the whole before he can seek to refine it.

374. It's one of the safest poisons you can die from.

[Sept. 1977; age 26]

375. Prediction: In the future dentists will not use x-rays. They will have a scanning device which by a 180 degree rotation will scan the entire tooth. This scan will be fed to a microcomputer which will display the tooth or teeth in three dimensions on a television screen. The dentist will be able to rotate the image any way he wishes. The image will also have color coding — for example, green for enamel, blue for fillings, red for cavities. (This prediction was made September 13, 1977. suggested by

current practice in computer axial tomography [color coded scan] and software manipulation of industrial designers [3-D rotating], and a dentist's complaint that x-ray angles can deceive one about the nature and extent of decay.)

376. Are you a heart specialist by education or by ego?

377. The ass knows not whether he bears gold or lead.

378. Picklock lived on Skeleton Quay.

379. Why do guides point out things that can't be seen? "The statue behind the tree is. . . ."

380. An ordinary blockhead I wouldn't mind, but he's a blockhead with termites.

381. Television and motion pictures are the great corrupters of morals and destroyers of intellect in modern society. They teach that arguments are to be solved by violence, that criminals are the real heroes, that adultery and fornication are as common and acceptable as iced tea, that the seemingly good are always corrupt, that all ministers are hypocrites or worse, and that the only objects worthy of pursuit are sex, money, idleness, and revenge.

382. Life is a great teacher. Write down the lessons you learn each day, whether from experience, observation, reading, a comment made by someone, a thought.

383. And now here's the latest hit by the Cold Stink.

384. Among the enemies of civilization, he ranks with those who eat fried chicken with their fingers while reading the classics borrowed from the library.

385. Was there anything to what he said, or was he just blowing

his nose on us?

386. Harold could tell she was a science major. When he asked her for a date, she did not say, "Never in a million years," she said, "Your chances approach zero in 10^6 years.

387. Try daily to
- Expand your horizons.
- Push back the frontiers of your knowledge.
- Seek improvements.
- Test innovations.
- Make advances.
- Recombine data.
- Move forward prayerfully but without hesitation.
- Preserve and enhance the excellent.

388. Darxul always held it among the first principles of wisdom that no man should open a book of criticism on an author until he had read the entire canon of the author's works twice. "If after a bite of the feast you leave the hall to study the history of feasting or the etiquette of table setting," he said, "then you will sit neither with the happy nor with the wise; you are destined for boredom, confusion, and hunger."

389. Gold weighs light in heaven.

390. All fire is accompanied by some smoke; it is therefore the very nature of the blazing fire of genius to produce a little cloudiness—some minimal smoke which obscures things here and there—and to allow in, unknowingly and unnoticed, a few flaws. Longinus knew this.

391. After you die, there will be no such question raised as, "Was he intelligent?" or "How long was his dissertation?" or "How many degrees did he have?" Rather, the question will be, "What did he do to serve God and to help mankind?"

392. One does not always see the future as clearly as one sees one's own nose, faults, or vain imaginations.

393. The best books are short books. We are mistaken in being impressed by fat, heavy volumes. We tend to assume offhand that a pagey book with small type is complete, learned, and thorough. This is wrong, for it only encourages the word pumpers. We ought to make our *a priori* assumptions resemble more nearly what we are really likely to find. We should lift the volume and remark, "Ugh! What a tub of blab is here! I wonder what an intolerably dull pack of unending verbiage has been crammed up between these covers. Surely there is a quicker way to make a doorstop, and an easier one to make outhouse sheets." My experience shows that the percentage of hot air and contrary winds in a book increases geometrically in proportion to its length. Further, big books are like big cows: they move slowly and undirectedly with a kind of squishy waddle. Who can tell where he goes in a sea of words? The author obviously cannot write an understandable sentence; for if he had been able to write clearly and concisely, we wouldn't now be plagued with this ship-sinking dead weight of his.

394. A very great danger in every search is not that you won't find what you are looking for, but that you will find the wrong thing first, apparently masquerading as the thing you seek. Anticipation, eagerness, and hope combine powerfully when we are looking for something; so much so that as soon as the seeming object appears, we have a strong tendency to seize it without further question or scrutiny. When one believes he has victory in his hands, it is difficult to withhold judgment until additional examination has yielded a positive, conclusive result.

Difficult, but it is necessary. We might characterize this overeager assumption of success as the Pounce Syndrome, since pouncing upon the object is what we do. The wrong object we might call, in some cases, a distracter, and in other cases, a poly. A distracter may be either planted or spontaneous.

Let us say the bomb squad is asked to search a building because saboteurs have been seen there. Unknown to the squad, the saboteurs have taken advantage of the Pounce Syndrome by planting two bombs — one easily located, the other well hidden. The first bomb — a planted distracter, and also a poly (i.e., multiple) in this case — will be easily found. The squad will pounce upon the bomb, and in the ensuing expenditure of satisfaction the squad members will find their further interest in bomb hunting defused. If they don't give up altogether, their further searching will be only half hearted. When we begin to search for "a" thing, and find "a" thing, we assume it is "the" (only) thing, when in actuality it may be either one of several things or the wrong, distracting imitation. (We are sold products this way).

In proofreading, although we know we look for more than one error, yet when we find one we pounce so ferociously that we often miss two or three errors in the nearby area. Our attention is temporarily defused by the gloat of satisfaction and triumph at our success.

A further problem arises from this. When happiness and satisfaction and rejoicing are expended on the wrong thing — the wrong winner, product, book, etc. — there is such an investment made emotionally that should the real item show up there will be no joy to spend on it (all has been expended) and, because of the emotional stake in the first item, the genuine object will be denied, and require much stricter proof of authenticity. Even then, the genuine thing may be a disappointment. Example — a reunion with a long lost relative; when the first arrives, high rejoicing — when the real one arrives, disbelief, unwillingness to displace the first, then less rejoicing.

395. Too much fiddling may be ruinous instead of perfective. Keep stirring and tasting and eventually you'll put in too much salt.

396. He has no second story — i.e., nothing upstairs.

397. Is "absolutely free" opposed to "partially free?"

398. Each age chastises all previous ages for their narrow views and dim perceptions, while erecting itself as the ultimate perceiver and interpreter of truth and reality.

399. If all you know is what you see on TV or read in the papers, you could scarcely be more ignorant or more prejudiced.

400. The practice of an art is to the rules governing it as ivy is to a trellis supporting it. The art, like the ivy, is living and free to grow and move. Only the trellis hidden beneath is rigid, silently guiding and shaping the art. The rules are a hidden support, not an overt mold or blueprint.

401. Our modern, moralless culture rejects old standards; now, whims which are stubbornly adhered to pass for values. Obstinacy is seen as a kind of virtue because it is the closest most people ever get to steadfastness.

402. The most fundamental disease of truth is a disease of the ear.

403. A bad book is a waste of money at any price, and a waste of time even if free.

404. Many people of violent opinions have never examined those opinions; there is always the fear that to examine them might change them. Whenever a large emotional investment is made in something, there is a reluctance to scrutinize it lest flaws be found showing it not to be worth the price.

405. How can a collection of evil, dissipated, and infidel quotations possibly help mankind?

406. To say that maxims and common-sense sayings should not be repeated because they are "hackneyed" or that they need not be repeated because they are true and obvious is to assert that the truth is hackneyed and obvious and need not be repeated.

Not only is this a false and objectionable assertion, but it leaves us only with new truths to be announced — not common in moral philosophy — and old falsehoods to be repeated. Most maxims are not clichés. He who argues they are shows his ignorance of maxims and proves that maxims need repeating.

407. Take courage; even if one day you must say, "I stand alone against five billion people and profess Jesus Christ," you are yet in the company of the hearts of believers from all ages — believers who looked forward to his coming for thousands of years and believers who now look forward to his coming again. And though you may be alone in the world, you will be together with God.

408. "What you see is what you get" is the wrong saying; what you labor tirelessly for is what you get.

409. What is the meaning of life? Purpose is what gives life meaning, and the purpose of life is to serve, please, and worship God.

410. The unities (time, place, action) are coherences whose purpose is to order a work — to make it like an organism: all one. If coherence can be established or maintained apart from one or more of the unities, the unity or unities can be (if desired) dispensed with.

411. Three hundred pages of runny-nose happy talk without ten coherent sentences or a single concrete suggestion. Why are textbooks — intended for education, I assume — written this way?

412. Semantic escape is the privilege of the learned. The ignorant cannot get away with it because they are not capable of disguising their equivocations with twelve-syllable words.

413. The deconstructionists and others would have us trample

upon hundreds or thousands of years of tradition to please their current ephemeral political whims. Tradition may be wrong—to hold to it thoughtlessly is certainly wrong—but a sudden decision to be displeased weighed against hundreds of years of harmony appears to be presumptuous, and a determined effort to hate, ridicule, and ostracize those who are happy and productive within the tradition is certainly vicious.

414. It is no wonder professors use the most complex terminology and obscure syntax possible; they all seem to have a horrible fear of sounding simplistic. A terrible condemnation is implied if a professor refers to an interpretation (even a 600 page one) as "somewhat oversimplified." How else is a non-specialist to understand? Is there an unspoken equation between truth and complexity? or between virtue and complexity? I think I will call my future books and writings, "X oversimplified." Perhaps I should change the name of this work to *Thoughts Oversimplified*. That way no professor will have to take his valuable time to call such a fact to the attention of his students.

415. It is possible eventually to arrive at truth by asking the wrong questions, but the way is so difficult, and roundabout, and fraught with errors, deceits, setbacks, missteps and confusions that any man will be well paid by choosing his questions with as much care as he uses when he sets about to answer them.

416. The only way to get their noses out of the clouds is to crack their kneecaps.

417. In my humble but correct opinion. . . .

418. I'm so wonderful that I don't have time to be egotistical.

419. Modern man is a victim of his own preconceived sneering. So much of past knowledge—of science, criticism, art, philosophy, and the Christian faith—is rejected abruptly and without

investigation because we have been taught to sneer before we have been taught to think.

420. Through the media the noisy elements of society are encouraging women to believe that men are enemies, oppressors, competitors, and selfish exploiters. Men are said to steal the identity of the girls they marry, deny them their "rights," and enslave them. Further, women are told that to be safe from the "menace of men" a hard, aggressive, suspicious, and distrustful behavior is necessary. From this it is no wonder our divorce rate is so high and that heterosexual harmony is low. A marriage, to be successful, must be built on trust and softness — it is an alliance. To "raise consciousness" this way and then lament divorce is like driving a wedge and lamenting the split.

421. Our age prides itself on scientific precision and exactness, and every worker in communications praises lucidity; but our practice shows that what we really want is squishy wording which will not be too limiting. The vague accommodates variety of beliefs, opinions, and interpretations, and therefore pleases more than the specific, which precludes certain opinions.

422. Being cheated is one of the inevitabilities of life on earth. Get used to it.

423. The marketing people won't allow us to be individuals because it is not as profitable as conformity. Mass market taste — in books, records, films, television programming — turns over many more dollars than would a widely splintered market. The trouble is, we are beginning to shape our tastes, beliefs, behavior, and dress even more quickly and easily to fit each new marketing fad.

424. My labors are as humble as the plowman's — mine are simply intellectual rather than physical.

425. A cosmic false analogy is being committed in modern socie-

ty by transferring the attitudes and practices of technology and consumption into the realm of values and culture. Rapidly outdated technology and the emphasis on the new and improved have put pressure on values and fixed ideals to yield to ever changing faddish ideas. The New, Improved Truth everyday replaces the Old, Lackluster Truth. The disposable products all around us encourage the feeling that relationships are also disposable and temporary. Yet security and the desire for permanence will always remain a basic human need.

426. What the advertisers are doing to us is not so strange or incomprehensible. They are merely appealing to five very basic sources of pleasure: novelty, excitement, energy, sex, and amazement. Consider the claims made for products. *Novelty*: New! Never Before! At last! Unusual! Different! Unique! *Excitement*: Wild! Fun! Exciting! The time of your life! Live a little! *Energy*: Powerful! Dynamic! Feel Great! *Sex*: a girl in a bikini with every purchase *Amazement*: Incredible! Wonderful! Amazing! Fantastic!

427. One regrettable shortcoming of literature is a lack of virtuous or heroic energetic characters. Energy is nearly worshipped by many people; villains are often destructively energetic; people wind up admiring villains.

428. He doesn't want to come home to a strutting, bold, opinionated, debating objector or to an economic, political, or jurisdictional competitor — he has these things when he does battle with the world. At home he wants an ally — softness, support, agreeableness, comfort, security, peace, relaxation.

429. "I was able to do it because I have a brilliant and analytical mind —"
    " — unhindered by modesty."

430. We're so smart — we've systematically rejected all the genuine stirrings of the spirit and told people that in an age of sci-

ence there can be no religion. But the old truism comes into play: "There is no such thing as no religion," and we worship science or worse, para-science—monsters, UFO's, psychic events, etc.

431. Wives, support your husbands; stand by their projects, dreams, hopes. Husbands, tell your wives you love them and need them and appreciate them.

432. My goal is to become a Christian Aristotle.

433. You can often measure the worth or excellence of your endeavors by the opposition they cause. Every great project has been vehemently opposed. To quote *Grit*: "Many great ideas have been lost because the people who had them couldn't stand being laughed at."

434. In hell, every way is down—to move is to go deeper.

435. To make a man better, hand him nothing but a book or a tool. All other free gifts will corrupt and degrade him.

436. Reaching toward grandeur or the sublime is related to the desire to feel or to express power. Corrupted, this reaching results in foolish and unachievable schemes.

437. If I waited for support to act, I'd die of old age in an unpropped bean field without a deed to my name.

438. We want—we need—direction in our lives. For arrows, sidewalks, well-worm paths we look to the ground. We ought to look to the stars.

439. There is no guilt in a single raindrop, but floods devastate homelands and kill hundreds.

440. Still stands the army of the infinite green, blades perched,

then order-threatening as a tuft of wind flexes the ranks.

441. Knowledge has been almost irremediably separated from enjoyment by the modern system of learning. Aristotle said, "All learning is accompanied by pain," and our modern educators are intent upon proving him true with a vengeance. The best method of instruction is, as Horace said, to teach *and* to delight. We should return to it.

442. The toast of knowledge is always burnt around the edges with ignorance, imprecision, and misinterpretation. We neither measure nor understand completely, yet we pretend to draw blueprints of the structure of the world. Real truth is revealed truth: our own readings of dirt, the heart, and the stars are stumbling mispronouncements.

443. Throughout the world there are humble and sincere Christians blessing and praising God, and we are members of the same flock.

444. Some say that pi before the Fall was 4.

445. We make too hasty an equation between perception and reality, and between analysis and reality. We think we can predict, or understand, or determine something, when sometimes we cannot even narrow a thing to its various possibilities.

446. When a substantial compliment enters the ear, the ego and the reason each seize an end and begin a great struggle over it. The ego insists that the compliment was sincere and is true; the reason pronounces the remark a piece of idle flattery, and at least exaggerated if not false in import. Which one wins this struggle shows the character of the man.

447. At least by frequent failure I know that I am trying to do something. There is some joy in the attempt and in the hope of success, though the flavor of failing is always the same—bitter.

Can one get used in time to eating alum?

448. What a man needs most from a wife is support and encouragement. A wife will do a large part of her duty to nurture her husband's dreams and protect and aid his delicate ego. To do these things, she must believe in her husband and in his ideas. No husband wants a false and dissimulating wife who merely says she agrees to please him—he wants genuine support. Thus, ladies, pick a man in whom you can believe, whose ideas seem right to you. That is a large part of compatibility.

449. The only thing faster than the speed of light is the flight of our hearts between hope and despair when we have some goal or wish in view about which there is some doubt of attainment. The vacillation is instant, and is repeated infinitely. The outcome, of course, remains entirely unaffected; we gain only fatigue, misery, and doubt. Human emotions are sometimes silly things.

450. We poor students must read so much that we have little or no time to think. As a consequence of the information explosion which buries us in books, we have a new paradox: we read too much to be wise. A lot of reading *of the right sort of books* is necessary to a full understanding of life; but endless perusal—volumetric acquisition—is counterproductive, because it makes the mind just a junkyard of thoughts and pieces of thoughts, burying each other and being buried among disordered scraps of ideas, prejudices, idiocies, wrong information, and truths. We need time to discover and assemble the truths, to identify and discard the junk ideas, and to understand why one is not the other.

451. Write something worthy to be cherished, to be savored; write words of such value that a reader, upon seeing them, will desire to tear them from the page and make them his—make them a part of his soul.

452. Thinking original and creative thoughts is difficult. What often passes for thinking is merely a continuous recirculation of two or three old ideas either in the same or different words. We play with one idea—mull it over, muse about it—but seldom strike upon a new idea.

453. Let me check my list of topics and think about something new. Let me pose a problem and solve it. A real problem of morals, ethics, being, purpose, etc., not an administrative technicality. Human romantic love is an administrative technicality.

454. I think I'm bit, but I've got a tourniquet on it, I think.

455. The presses are growing hungrier, but at the same time do we have less and less worthwhile material to communicate? Technology is daily improving communications, from print to satellite, but what fills the available capacity? Junk too often is created to supply the need—we need 800 books a year at our publishing house; we need an hour of "news" events every day for our station. The hunger would be good if it had a varied fare to satiate it, if books of all kinds, persuasions, etc. could have opportunity. But we find instead a menu of single entrees. The press, the video media, can no longer digest cultural variety or intellectual challenge. Novels, for example, are so little varied from the standard that they could be—maybe are—put out by computer, and the people are so used to buying and processing this pulp that they themselves would probably resist any new or different materials.

456. On one level it is true that a woman is nothing but a bag of guts and muscles covered with skin and hair; on one level it is true that a house is nothing but a box made of boards and cement, all not too carefully assembled; and on one level it is true that when you get married and buy a house, you have done nothing but gain a personal bag of guts and a box in which to live with it. But what has really happened is that you have found an intelligence to throw in with you, an ally to help create

an other worldly existence within the walls of your castle. That bag of guts is a supernatural being with the magic power to enable you to resist the viciousness, antagonism, and onslaughts of the entire world. Her support, reassurance, agreeableness, and easy-going nature heal every wound from the battle of life, and empower you to charge — not simply to return to the fight, but to charge — every day with every confidence. And that little box is really an enchanted forest where the battle of life takes a pause; a verdant spot free from the stress of competition, the demands, disagreement, and condemnation of the world at large. You walk through the door to be greeted by the enchantress of the wood, who offers you encouragement and belief to counteract the evil spells of an undercutting and unbelieving world. You take your shoes off, she lets her hair down, and you embrace a dream.

457. Think through the implications of your work before releasing it.

458. Why has the twentieth century trivialized the important and made important the trivial? And again, why are we general when we ought to be specific and specific when we ought to be general?

459. Faith and trust are necessary for sanity.

460. The mouth is involved in learning. When you study, you should also chew gum, sip water, eat lifesavers, put a pencil in your mouth, purse your lips, pinch them.

461. Most people act largely from the pleasure principle rather than from intellectual principles. Thus, instilling in them an intellectual aversion to evil will not be very effective in reforming their behavior. What must be done to reduce or eliminate evil is to destroy the sensations or associations of pleasure accompanying the evil. Ridicule is here an effective weapon, and satire its vehicle. Not even the devil can stand to be laughed at. Associate

a vice with scornful, contemptuous, humiliating laughter in an individual's mind and you will cure that vice in him. Reason seldom effects practical change because people seldom act on reason.

462. Teach the difference between depth and obscurity and you will have helped to cure one of the major errors of modernism.

463. The general complexity of modern life has caused us to commit a giant fallacy of accident: because so many things require complex or sophisticated explanations, we have become convinced that all things must have these kinds of explanations. The result is preference for the oversophisticated explanation, even at the expense of truth and reason. An anti-Occam's Razor sentiment pervades our attitudes, and we attack easy and straightforward answers as "too simplistic," when in reality there is much truth in simplicity. The ultimate result of this insistence on complexity is the creation of false, affected, implausible — but impressive — reasons and causes.

464. We are always confusing our minds and wasting our hours contemplating *improbable* possibilities, while we remain blind to the *real* possibilities which have some hope of being achieved. "Expand your thoughts to the possibilities for your life," say the sages, and immediately we begin to think of ridiculous schemes, chance events, Fortune's unstoppably rising wheel — all possible events, but so unlikely as to render the thought of their occurrence vain and dissipating: waiting for them is idle and demoralizing; trying to bring them about is wasteful and frustrating. We should instead concentrate on the genuine possibilities which we often do not recognize. We are so trained after a life of disappointment to reject all possibilities as fanciful except those wild ones we indulge for mental recreation or egotism, that we seldom allow ourselves to see what we really might expect to accomplish. But we ought to dream real dreams — dreams which can be made real. As Longinus says, "Even in orgies of the imagination it is necessary to remain so-

ber." Which possibilities have opportunity and statistical signif-icance on their side?

465. Use neither too many nor too few words to convey your ideas. Concision at the expense of fullness or clarity is as great a vice as verbosity.

466. People seem to have a feeling of inadequacy or of low abil-ity, and therefore are willing to accept something less than true excellence in art, because even the mediocre work appears be-yond their abilities. A few praise the low because they aspire to it, and realize that true excellence is beyond them — too much work or too much talent is required.

467. If you want to be an artist of the first and best kind, study the best works in your field as models: imitate them; try even-tually to surpass them. (To surpass Bach or Handel or Beetho-ven, for example, would be quite an accomplishment.) Educate yourself about the rules, practices, procedures, fundamentals of your art. Art is a product of skill, education, diligence and most-ly plain hard work. Art does not spring spontaneously from the gut in finished form. Even the Romantic poets like Shelley la-bored over their verses, while claiming spontaneity.

468. **False Assumptions Corrected.**
    A. People are reasonable and act from the principles of rea-son. (Most people follow urges, whims, and emotional stirrings, and neither listen to reason nor allow it to play a major role in their daily lives and actions.)
    B. People can discern truth from falsehood. (Most people are extremely ignorant of the facts necessary to determine the just-ness of any given statement; these people therefore rely on what is popular or commonly accepted or considered proper to be-lieve. Liberals are especially gullible this way. Other people ac-cept whatever is repeated often enough, as in the news media. Knowledge and reason joined in independent thinking are nec-essary to determine truth, and even then some failures will re-

sult.)

C. Truth will triumph over falsehood if they are left alone. (Falsehood has the advantages of ignorance, emotional prejudices, self-interested knaves, ease of belief, and popularity. The devil is always spreading it to willing ears. Truth is frequently unpleasant, requires knowledge, and is unpopular. An old cliché tells us, "The truth hurts," and so we resist it. Very few are natural lovers of truth: to become one for the rest of us takes a firm resolution and a stern discipline.)

469. The command to charge, spurs, a gallop. Firing. Noise, smoke, confusion. Blood boiling past your ears, adrenalin through the guts, stomach tight, heart pounding, hairs stiff on end, the air dense with the smell of blood and dirt, horse and rider nostrils flared, teeth, dirt flies, blood spurts, metal, horses running strange slow motion, falling, men running, falling, screaming shell, disjointed, screams, animal noises, joints and tendons popping, visible, somewhere a bugle. Down, the dirt, am I wounded, rifles, cannons, the ground blasted, the ground rising and falling, vibration, dust, men down, are we winning, confusion, smoke, noise.

470. "What can't be got by the mind must be got by the sweat." —Proverb.

471. The secret of success is gaining enough speed on the downhill slopes to reach the top of the hill.

472. What mortals overlook shall God take note of twice.

473. The road to hell is indeed paved with good intentions but the floor of hell is paved with people who too often used that quotation in lieu of action.

474. I have an answer for every question. Usually, though, the answer is, "I don't know."

475. It is impossible to cherish quantity. All love is for individual members. He who loves a quantity loves the concept of largeness for its own sake only. People who make seemingly quantity generalizations—"I love music" or "I love the museum's gem collection" are summarizing their feelings toward individual pieces.

476. We think we are big and strong, but we can be driven indoors by a single, persistent, little gnat buzzing about our ears and eyes.

477. He who has an answer for everything has many useless answers.

478. Doctors, lawyers, and professors are all practitioners of mechanic arts, and are all in service industries. They are essentially the same kind of workers as plumbers, auto mechanics, and air conditioner repairmen. They need slightly more education, but that should not give them exalted egos. And how little of their ideals, over which they get so puffed up—do we see in practice. A professor is supposed to be the protector, transmitter, and encourager of culture, but instead ignores it or tears it down. A doctor is supposed to serve humanity but instead wants only money and four days a week off. A lawyer is supposed to insure "equal justice under law." No comment needs to be made about the farce of that.

479. It used to be that when a girl and a boy got together, they would play; now they compete. This does not bode well for happy marriages. Modern women have no concern for the male ego, which being weaker than the female ego, is very easily damaged. When a power struggle begins—whether one for ego dominance, one of economic competition (both spouses working), or even of sporting competition, a wedge is driven between the two who are supposed to be one. We no longer see one helping and supporting and securing the other, but rather one pitted against the other. Marriage should offer a relief from

the struggle of the world, not merely an extension and intensification of the struggle.

480. The promoters of evil are even more frightened and insecure than the supporters of virtue. Though evil is very successful, it is always on the brink of destruction. If the virtuous would persevere in spite of fear and uncertainty, they would remoralize the world.

481. Certainly God feels emotions. We are wrong to say he is "pure reason" if that means he does not feel. He is not cold but warm hearted. He can feel anger, pity, sorrow, joy, love, sympathy, disappointment (see the account of the flood), and happiness.

482. To be loyal to another person is to give up a part of yourself to him and to subordinate part of yourself to him.

483. Women's Lib has a lot of genuine misanthropy in it. I've never met a genuine misogynist—a man who really hated all women—but I have met several women who hate men in general and who hold men in contempt.

484. The words "duty," "dependent," "serve," "subordinate," and "yield" are looked upon now with disdain, hatred, and contempt. That is the sign of a selfish age. Our age has witnessed the triumph of the self-oriented philosophy—for example, feminism, the new morality, government for me, expediency, etc.

485. The people who "hold the public trust" and are supposed to be knowledgeable, reasonable, and fair, are really more ignorant, capricious, and unjust than the least distinguished of common citizens.

486. The traffic on our freeways is getting almost as heavy as that on the road to hell.

487. As for Harold, he went home and oiled his garage-door hinges.

488. The problem with many students' thinking is not that they back their opinions with the wrong reasons, but that they back them with no reasons. And opinions welded into the guts are much more difficult to change than those riveted into the mind, unless the gut opinions are replaced by equally ridiculous ones. That's why so many students are such rabid canaries when they emerge from the university.

489. Be careful when everyone begins shouting in one direction: it means that no one is looking around.

490. The quality of life is advanced by appropriate education (the training of taste, intellect, reason, emotional expectations) and by the presence of good aesthetics (environment, safety, decoration, art).

491. Women's lib derives its strength from being a cult of the self in a selfish age—hence the antagonism toward love, which is a selfless and dependent emotion.

492. Being a Californian, he was born with a silver car key in his mouth.

493. Flimsy thinking, flimsy morals; flimsy morals, flimsy laws, flimsy laws, flimsy society; flimsy society, flimsy education; flimsy education, flimsy thinking.

494. People are too concerned generally with seeking personal solutions, when they should be seeking others' solutions in larger contexts, and thereby laboring to advance the quality of life and civilization of all mankind.

495. Not coincidentally, we too often make assumptions which are agreeable with our will or desires rather than with strict

probability. This creates a twofold disappointment when the assumption proves false.

496. The giver of goods or help is in a natural position of superiority over the receiver, and the receiver admits an inferior position by accepting the gift. The inferiority is not necessarily significant and is seldom of much importance—the inferiority shown by someone who accepts a stick of chewing gum, a loan or gift of a few dollars, or who asks someone to change a flat is not very great. The sense of inferiority arises powerfully only in the minds of the aggressive, independent types who are almost angrily determined never to be dependent upon anyone for anything, no matter how much suffering must be involved. Humans are dependent beings; giving help or gifts is a pleasure; being indebted is often a strengthener of relationships. These facts are ignored or denied by the "independent."

497. The Flibs discourage love and tokens of male affection because the tokens smack of female submissiveness and male dominance. Love involves a desire to help, to take care of, to have the beloved *submit* to your aid; thus love is indeed a dependent relationship. The Flibs want *independence*, even if it means being heartless, uncaring, and selfish. They don't want to love or to be loved; they want only intellectual respect. I saw a quotation recently, attributed to "Women's Liberation: Notes from the Second Year." It was, "We must destroy love. . . . Love promotes vulnerability, dependence, possessiveness, susceptibility to pain, and prevents the full development of woman's human potential by directing all her energies outward in the interest of others." If this is a typical or general belief, it certainly is a Q.E.D. to my discussion. The Flibs are self-oriented; love is other-oriented.

498. Women, be agreeable and tender; you will improve the world significantly.

499. We are easily deceived by imitations of familiar patterns or

by circumstances which appear to fit known patterns. We see a partial pattern—we think—and our minds fill in the blanks and reconcile difficulties; in our passion for order and consistency we lead ourselves astray and distort the truth.

500. We are suspicious of the strange, not of the familiar. Plain sight hides best.

501. A predisposition or determination to agree or to disagree has more effect on the perception, progress, and outcome of an argument than real differences or similarities have.

502. Spending ten dollars to save a hundred is a bargain, but more often we spend ten dollars to save five.

503. Occasionally we persevere past the solution. We get so caught up in doing battle and struggling toward the goal, that we pass the goal by.

504. The motor gets the credit for doing the work, but the starting switch got the motor going. Plant seeds.

505. It is indeed the heart which needs to be changed to allow in the Christian faith, but the direct route is difficult and only one possibility. By my knocking out the props from under selfishness, by exposing the flimsy philosophical framework behind worldliness, perhaps the heart will be encouraged to look around for a new center of gravity.

506. How important is the job of an intermediary, who relays the truth from the source to the object? Through relays, a micro switch can make an 80,000 horsepower pump fill a lake to water a thirsty city.

507. We must not get carried away with the categories we create. While there are emotional, spiritual, intellectual and philosophical areas or "parts" of the human psyche, man cannot be

rigidly divided and one part is not independent of the others. Thus, for example, a change in philosophy affects the emotions, a darkened spirit affects the way a person thinks and reasons, an emotional change can change philosophy, intellect, or even religious faith—more so in people who live by their guts.

508. Why are people so callous? You cannot grow mushrooms in a burning barn.

509. We say, "That's simplistic," when its true complexities are beyond our power; we say, "That's complex," when we cannot understand its true simplicity. We think we understand subtlety, profundity, metaphor, extension, and application. We also dream when we sleep.

510. It *is* possible to reach the heart through the intellect, and vice versa.

511. Spiders are the signifiers of neglect or desertion. What man abandons, spiders will use.

512. If we can once crack the shell of their worldliness, the Holy Spirit will find his way in.

513. Horace's dictum on art—*dulce et utile*—can be extended to effectiveness of teaching. An aesthetic recommendation of truth is a more effective persuader than a blunt statement because both truth and art extend from the mind into the soul. Thus for example, the truth set to a penetrating melody or couched in the form of poetic excellence is much more readily accepted since it covers the entire framework of the human understanding. Advertisers have abused this phenomenon by adding jingles to their messages in an attempt not only to brainwash us, but to soul wash us as well.

514. What objectors often lack is understanding. Before you object to a statement or position, ask the speaker a question, fram-

ing what you believe to be his position in your own words, and see if he assents to it. You thereby will assure yourself that you understand what you are objecting to; you also allow the speaker to hear his views from another party and provide him an opportunity to explain or amend them. Do not tell someone what he believes; ask him if it is so.

515. People get lost in unfamiliar territory because they neglect — or refuse — to follow the map. Maps — good maps — have been given, invented, discovered, or empirically constructed for guidance in every realm of our being. And they are tried and proven guides. God's map, for example, has been with us for thousands of years, and every day, both by the effects upon those who follow it and by the effects upon those who don't, it has shown its worth and truth. Taking no map, but following each road that attracts you, guessing at your route, imagining your destination, or going about aimlessly may please you for awhile, but you'll eventually wind up lost and miserable. You can change your heart now and accept Christ as your guide, or you can wait until your heart, in its pain, will change you.

516. It is harder to defend ourselves against our friends than against our enemies because we assume that our friends have no antipathy toward us, and that their objections are sincere and reasoned rather than antagonistic. This disarms us, and we take their criticisms and objections more to heart, assuming that our friends have a sympathetic understanding of our beliefs. While in argument with genuine opponents we tend to keep our own positions more fully in view, in arguments with our friends we sincerely try to understand their position. As a result, ignorance or misinformation on their part about our beliefs confuses us; they attack what is not really our position, yet our respect for them recommends the words and we become at a loss for an answer — for who has answers to attacks on positions he does not hold?

517. A good wife should be understanding; though not simply

understanding, but sympathetic; and not simply sympathetic, but an ally; and not simply an ally, but a primary encourager to action, a main support, a believer in the cause.

518. God loves even boring stick-in-the-muds.

519. Not all truth is permanent or eternal, even aside from opinion masquerading as truth. For example, "His watch is waterproof" may be true now, but not true in ten years. Truths, to be valuable guides, then, must be tested by time. Every generation has objected to God's truth, and yet by testing it has proved it enduringly true.

520. All mental faculties are interrelated, so that by encouraging immoral behavior and by intellectual ridicule, the educational establishment *consciously* attempts (and succeeds) to erect a permanent barrier to religious belief. The Gospel is rejected out of hand, not as being wrong religiously or emotionally, but as being inconsistent with modern moral and intellectual attitudes. Hence, the fake religions like TM are all right, because they do not interfere with or make claims upon the morals and the intellect.

521. Perhaps we have done too much dividing. We divide to learn, but we should reassemble to understand. All things are one, in some sense at least. We as humans are each one, however inconsistent. We cannot for long alienate one part from the others. That's why self denial is a good for the whole— foregoing extra food or fasting helps not just the body, but the mind, the soul, the heart.

522. Books and theories may not be completely or even largely true, but don't quit reading and cast them aside, for there may be something of the truth there upon which you can build. A partial explanation with some inaccuracies or errors may still be useful as a starting point to reach the pure and perfect truth.

523. Many of our attitudes and beliefs are products of our experience; and our experience, individually, is seldom justly representative of real life in general. We all have had a series of unique and often bizarre or atypical episodes in our lives. To generalize about life from such experiences thus creates an enormously distorted picture—a hasty generalization of the worst sort, because we order and direct our lives and behavior on their basis. Ask yourself about your attitudes towards men, women, the poor, the rich, boy scouts, the police, etc, etc. and make an attempt to determine the exact basis for your views. Are your experiences really typical?

524. We want to be individuals—that is, atypical—and yet have normal—that is, typical—experiences.

525. "You can't argue with success." You certainly can if it's short-term success, because that is fifty percent marketing and fifty percent caprice and fad. And both marketing and fad are products or involve logical fallacies: marketing is often based on brainwashing (repetition) and fad on the *ad populum* appeal. Real worth, value, taste and so forth are not at all necessary for short term success.

526. All things are interrelated. One's life philosophy affects his job quality. Morality can lead to spirituality. Art affects behavior.

527. To deter the wicked from hurting the innocent serves God greatly, though only in a "moral" and not a spiritual way. For the sake of our Christian witness, for the sake of other believers, for the sake of those who may become believers, for the sake of our love toward all men, for the sake of our own happiness, for the sake of God's commandments, we must always demonstrate visibly our hatred and contempt for vice and evil.

528. A journey of a thousand miles starts with pushing your wife out of bed to make the coffee. —Proverb.

529. Lessons learned from dismantling and studying the guts of a mechanical adding machine.

1. Comprehension must begin with a close focus on the smallest relationships. An overview shows broad actions, but the real relationships remain obscure until only the interactions of two parts are studied. A group of men, or society in general, can best be understood by examining the connections between individuals. One effect may require a thousand causal steps.

2. Complexity consists in multiplied simple relationships and steps. A complex goal — whether of making, doing, under-standing — can be achieved by breaking down the path to that goal into simple steps.

3. Each part — in society, business, the environment — touches many other parts either directly or by necessary action. In some cases, a part may fail without very much effect; but most often, the failure of a part is like the breaking of a link in a chain — the whole subsystem, and perhaps even the overall machine, will fail or be seriously compromised.

4. Certain springs and certain levers are invisible to the operator of the machine. They are, however, equally as important (that is, essential) to the proper printing of the answer as are the number printing bars which the operator can see leaping into action at every push of a button.

5. The screws never move — but they hold the universe together. "They also serve who only stand and wait."

6. [Story: "It's Nut Valuable," published on the Web on Vir-tualSalt.com, in *Stories from the Old Attic* (1992), and in *Seventy Stories and a Poem* (2013)].

7. A mechanical memory is exact, firm, permanent until erased. It does not confuse or interchange facts, but always keeps order and precision. Yet it can do nothing with the facts except hold, yield, add, subtract, etc. at the command of others. There is no creativity, no metaphor.

8. A lot of the parts are the same — ten or twelve of this, twenty of that. But the sameness does not diminish their value. A part with ten others exactly like it is entirely as essential as a

unique part.

530. To reject a combination does not imply rejection of its components. I like spinach, dill pickles, coffee ice cream, cheese, and cranberry juice; but I would not want them together in a pie.

531. Consistency is a test of truth, but not in human behavior, for people are by nature often inconsistent in their actions.

532. Stating a matter in a parable allows people to judge the morality or justice of the thing without the interference of self interest or personal prejudices. Cf. Matthew 21:33 ff, where the Pharisees condemn themselves.

533. Learning causes insanity—or at least it can cause a kind of unsoundness of mind. These sometimes ruinous effects of education can be divided into stages.

In the first stage, the learner becomes egotistical, self satisfied, and contemptuous of the understanding of others. He becomes intolerant of the ideas of others and judges most things negatively before inquiring into them.

In the second stage, our learner grows cold, loses the feelings of affection and personal warmth, and becomes insensitive, unkind, and highly disagreeable. He objects to others' ideas without regard to feelings or use of tact. He begins to grow aggressive and more and more bigoted.

In the third stage, a general boredom with life has set in, and the highly educated person now feels vaguely unhappy and discontent. He is almost completely detached from "ordinary life" or "the real world"; he is haughty, snobbish, condescending. At the same time, he is addle headed in his thinking, both practically and theoretically. He has become incompetent to function on a practical level because he has for so long spurned non-ideal things. There has been a complete split between ideals and application, and the only world he knows is one of impossible theory, to which he clings vehemently. His human relationships are false, plastic, awkward, unsatisfying. The emotions of love, kindness, sympathy, and so forth have all been crushed. Only anger and hatred remain. He cannot enjoy simple pleasures—a bouquet of flowers, a rest on the grass; he demands that everything be significant, even though a lot of life isn't.

In the fourth stage, the overlearned has become a reclusive, misanthropic, bitter atheist, harboring a contempt for everything except for the facts and the "creators" of those facts in which he is interested. He collects knowledge like a miser collecting money—with no plans to make any use of it, and without doing himself any good. (For knowledge is like money; some people do not know how to use it.)

534. Be willing to fail and nothing can stop you.

535. And behold, their works were dross in the blast furnace of the Lord.

536. The kinds of women who "want" things—who always seem to be after something—have inspired an age old question: Just what is it that a woman wants? The search for an answer has been complicated by the fact that few of these women will clearly admit even to themselves, much less to others, what they are after. But I think I have the answer, based on much observation, a lot of thought, and some reading. The answer is: power. Not fame or glory—men's big desire. Often social and economic, sometimes political. But really more fundamental—a power of dominion and sphere rule, accompanied by a desire to display and extend it.

537. You can cram your guts with a good quantity of wishes and still be hungry.

538. Modern definitions of fun and recreation all seem to imply a rather high level of adrenalin in the blood. Quiet pleasures, however exciting, are snubbed.

539. And as for Kathy, she went home, grabbed her little cassette recorder, got into a hot bath, and listened to Handel's *Water Music*.

540. Be careful not to become preprejudiced by an image or a reputation. When you see something, or are presented with a situation, do not ask, How do I perceive this, but, What is its true nature? Don't ask, What does this seem to be—half the world is seeming to be something else—but ask instead, What is this? The simplest example of the necessary distinction between appearance and reality is in consumer products—for example, Marlborough Cigarettes used to be for women, and are now for rugged men—by a change of seeming. How sad it is to be duped and manipulated by the surfaces and externals of the world, yet how few of us manage to escape the power of the image makers. As Shakespeare said, "Hypeness is all."

541. I'm as anxious to taste the grapes as any man, but I don't expect to have the run of the vineyard until after the deed is signed.

542. We must indeed take care to avoid obstacles and problems, but we need perhaps as great a care to assure that, while avoiding one bad thing, we don't inadvertently draw close to or jump into the lap of another.

543. We are suffering enormously today at the hands of those who insist on fitting facts to a theory which neither explains nor has any relation to the facts. The theories of evolutionists, psychologists, sociologists, economists, women's libbers, politicians, criminologists, and so on usually seem to result from the theorizer's desire to see his preconceptions realized rather than from an inductive generalization really related to observation and measurement. Those in power—as scientists, teachers, textbook writers, media feeders—are not different from ordinary types who sometimes fall into a fit, desiring violently that something should be true or false when it stubbornly really isn't. The

difference is that those in power just ignore the true state of things and cry up their scenario, interpretation, or judgment of what ought to be, calling it the real truth. And the three most powerful persuaders are not logic, experiment, and historical fact, but the material fallacies of repetition, appeal to prestige, and appeal to the masses—that is, people believe a statement because it has been repeated often, has been spoken by the famous or powerful, and is generally in everybody's mouth.

544. One of the problems of being eighteen is having all the answers, none of which are correct.

545. A lot of people, even on the level of the very educated, define themselves by contradicting or disagreeing with whatever others say. Disagreeing is encouraged now because it supposedly shows that you are thinking for yourself, and, of course, it also gives you a feeling of superiority, since it shows that you believe your knowledge and wisdom superior on a particular point. I do not encourage you to disagree; I encourage you to think. More often than is let on, thinking for yourself results in agreement—even in this wrong headed age.

546. "Why get married? A marriage certificate is only a piece of paper." This is true. Also true: the Constitution is only a piece of paper; thousand-dollar bills are only pieces of paper; the classics of Greece and Rome are only pieces of paper; the Bible is only a bunch of pieces of paper. Don't bother to give me a deed to the property; a deed is only a piece of paper.

547. Often the difference between a plain old fly out and a home run is only a matter of ten feet. Just a little more effort—a little more push—would have made the difference.

548. No wonder advertisers use logical fallacies to sell products; people have an amazing ability to ignore reason. Swaying their guts makes them act; reasoning with their minds makes them sleep. There are implications here for jury trials.

549. The best poetry and the best music balance predictability (patterns) against novelty and surprise.

550. I dislike the life of a scholar pedant because I want to talk about ideas—not about opinions of interpretations of implications of ideas.

551. Love and friendship are not alone sufficient for a smooth and happy interactive marriage. A very important quality needed is personality compatibility. Other attractions (intellectual, physical, spiritual) can change, flex, or grow more rapidly, and can be harmonized more easily. But the personality program—an almost subconscious behavior, attitude, and response system—changes much more slowly, if it changes at all. And because it involves the mechanics of emotional and intellectual coexistence, it determines perhaps to a greater extent than the regular attractions, how well two people will get along over time. (It can be flexed or suppressed briefly enough to maintain casual friendships.)

552. I just noticed that Glimmering #534 is an amphibology of sorts. I meant to say, in a few words, that only by being willing to fail, and therefore by being willing to take a chance, would you be able to proceed to the task which would result in success. "Nothing can stop you" from succeeding if you are willing to chance failing.

553. One of the major purposes of knowledge is action. "Knowing is half of life." — Proverb. "Practicing what you know is the other half of life." — Another Proverb. Our action should not be purposely confined to a small sphere, but should be spread into as large a realm as we can manage. Improve, help, reform, save the whole world if you can. Knowledge, worthy to be possessed by us is worthy for others to possess. Spread it.

554. In the human sector, noise is usually made in inverse pro-

portion to power.

555. Marriage should be a lifelong and permanent commitment, because it is the physical manifestation or the physical portion of a spiritual truth, commitment, and relationship. Marriage is the earthly, tangible, physical, human representation of God's love, not altering or removing with changes in time, situation, or behavior. In our personal spiritual lives, we know that whatever happens in the transitoriness of worldly values, beliefs, morals, events, there is a secure rock of Christian Biblical faith. The permanence and stability of that faith give us intellectual and spiritual security. Similarly, in our marriage relationship, we know that whatever happens in social interaction — rejection, failure, hate, opposition — or in the physical world around us — sickness, property loss, crime, war — there is a secure rock of a committed Christian marriage offering support, acceptance, help, and love. The permanence and stability of the marriage bond give us emotional and physical security. The Christian marriage combining these four kinds of security — intellectual, spiritual, emotional, physical — provides the best contribution available to man toward his happiness, stability, sanity, productivity, and health.

556. The difference between a pile of worthless junk and a pile of worthy raw materials is often one of vision and attitude rather than one of substance.

557. Justice and mercy can be demonstrated and understood through the applications of law and theory, because they (justice and mercy) are intellectual concepts. But love, while it can be defined and explained intellectually, is best demonstrated and understood through a personal relationship. The Old Testament shows us justice and mercy, but Christ in the flesh demonstrated love.

558. The incarnation was necessary to explain several points left unclear by the "law and the prophets." These include:

1. What is God really like, as a being with whom man can interact and communicate? We have his law and his deeds in the O.T., but how are we to relate to and talk to him directly, as we should with a father?

2. What does God really mean by *love*? Love is an interpersonal commitment, involving exchange and concern, action, and non-verbal communication. Love must be presented in person, and not by writ.

3. How can man be like God? How can we imitate a creator whom we have not seen, and whose ways and actions we cannot sense?

4. What price or sacrifice is God willing to give for man, and what is the tangible evidence for that sacrifice or price?

The people with the invisible God had an opportunity to behold him, to study his ways, to observe a model for imitation, and to sense, at least in a small way, the price he would pay for them.

559. Importance and value are given to a thing (object or person) by time and by acquaintance with or knowledge about it. The two value givers usually work together, so that acquaintance over a period of time renders almost anything significant. Advertisers repeat slogans and show off products over a long ad campaign to increase perceived value. The familiar has value, just because it is familiar and because we will therefore prefer it to the unknown. A fictional character in a film will have value according to his presence in the film (acquaintance over time). If he comes on screen suddenly and is killed, we attach little importance to him and our emotions are not disturbed except to the extent that the killing disturbs us when any person is killed. If, however, the character has been developed for an hour of close attention, and is then killed, we are much more sensible, because the death seems much more significant — we have given importance, if not value, to the character because we know him.

Trivial things can become invested with apparent value if we concentrate on them over a long period of time, and neglect to look up for a minute to find our reference points. Thus, we find the pedantic scholar wrestling with a punctuation mark for thirty years, the adolescent turning a small disappointment into a life crisis, and the hopeful scientist or gullible investigator inflating a tiny clue into a giant proof of absolute certainty. Indeed, depression frequently has been caused by the inflation of the trivial, thinking over and over about a fault, error, or missed opportunity. The repetition—the acquaintance over time—creates the perception of value or significance in the event.

560. Naturally, of course, in these Modern Times, in Today's Society, now that we have *really* arrived, Plato's allegory of the cave is no longer relevant. This is an age of high technology—we could never be deceived by mere shadows. We have electronics. We can now know the Truth. We turn on the radio, and listen to the lightning static, and are convinced that the noise is real lightning and real thunder. If it's electronic, it must be true. No shadows for us.

561. This is an age of surfaces. We are afraid to discuss important issues except on a cliché level. Thinking hurts. We are safer and more comfortable on the surface. But all things are interrelated, and this superficiality has created the age of the symptomatic cure—for medical problems, psychological aberrancies, drug abuse, crime, poverty. We plaster the surface rather than try to discover an inner cause. If you are unhappy, go to a movie or dance to cheer up—or take dope. If you take dope, switch to a substitute "feel good" drug. Our modern solution for unwanted pregnancy is abortion, not birth control; we try to cure VD by counseling for check ups, not chastity. Perhaps we have given up on the true solutions because we don't believe they will work. If we believe that, they won't.

562. Every project should have secondary goals which can be effected even if the primary goal of the project fails, so that the energy, effort, and time spent on a project will not be entirely wasted when the primary goal cannot be achieved. This strate-

gy can be further advantageous in those frequent cases where secondary goals become more important and where the original goal becomes unimportant, useless, unnecessary or undesirable. New information sometimes renders original goals obsolete or even dangerous. It is easier in such cases to redirect energies into associated channels or at least into areas prepared for earlier, than to halt, regroup, back up, and start again in a new direction. If a single plan is pursued and then defeated, you are stopped until you can regroup, replan, and redeploy. If you have a plan with one or more contingency plans, and if you expect the possibility of defeat or change, the defeat of the main plan will merely redirect or detour you. Advance planning when you are cool, relaxed, and reasonable should always be preferred to a pressed decision made in the face of defeat.

563. Our preconceptions sometimes rule us to such an extent that evidence contrary to or inharmonious with them must be immense and overpowering before we will even consider the possibility of "misbelief" on our part. We even filter, distort, or change completely some perceptions to make them fit our preconceived ideas, and then pat ourselves on the back for being right all along. Thus, hunting for proof of a theory—whether it be evolution, UFO's or your own pet notion—is extremely hard on the facts, detrimental to the cause of truth, and often successful in the eyes of the investigator. "A man will believe anything he tells himself." —Proverb.

564. Glimmerings #561 and #563 together show us that society now displays an increasing inability to see past exteriors *because* it does not want to see past them. There is a convenience in pretending that the external is the real: such a pretense makes us "wise," because a quick look and a handful of stereotypes are all that is necessary to "understand" life.

565. "Knowledge puffeth up." True, but *imagined* knowledge puffeth men up even more, to the endless amusement of those who appreciate irony. Knowing something certainly gives no

cause for egotism, but merely thinking one knows something, or believing that the wrong thing is knowledge, and then getting puffed up about it—what a creature is man.

566. Erasers and locks are the great symbols of modern man.

567. Temptations are usually either tangible or have some tangible result, while the morals and spirituality with which to resist those temptations are intangible ideals. And we are sensuous creatures. So we succumb. "The spirit is willing but the flesh is weak."

568. The evil, the immoral, the expedient, the lovers of pseudo philosophically inflated trivia, the materialists, the feelies—all are constantly pressuring us to distort or abandon our values and morals, our hierarchies and priorities. They pretend that faith does not now exist, and that it is contemptible that it even did exist. There is a strong movement to make economic values (money) outweigh moral virtues, and to make pragmatic and expedient reasons outweigh philosophical and ideal reasons. We are moving from the ideal to the material, from the spiritual to the carnal. Money and goods answer every objection: sell your virtue, and gain money, abort your baby and save money; choose your life's work based on the income you'll get from it. These pressures work on us subtly as well as overtly, so that we must be careful to maintain our ideals consciously and firmly— even repeating them if necessary to overcome the brainwashing of the world—or we will be seduced into the exaltation of freighted inanities and evanescent beacons.

569. Fact and truth are not coextensive. By excessive concentration on issues capable of empirical determination we are limiting our knowledge and understanding of the universe—and of ourselves. Truth is much broader and more profoundly significant than fact. A flower's color and number and shape of petals are facts, but its beauty and uniqueness are truths of a higher order. You plant a seed and it grows. That's a fact. But the mira-

cle of unfolding life—a flower exploding from a seed—symmetry, softness, color, and proportion rising from a dry hard particle—there is a truth in that, about life and creation, which no empiricist can show.

570. "One think leads to another." —Proverb. This is a promise and a warning.

571. Once in a pleasant garden there stood a tree, from which, legend said, God himself would one day reign. But instead, a bunch of wicked men broke in and chopped the tree down. They hacked the tree into a beam and nailed a holy man to it, leaving him to die up on a hill. So the tree of hope now had become a beam covered with blood and death. See here, the wicked men said, laughing to scorn, in what manner God's promises are fulfilled.

572. We live in a coherent universe, where actions and events have coherent causes and effects. Those who deny this truth wish to excuse capricious and inconsistent behavior.

573. The more our society acclaims the power, rights, and nobility of the individual, the stronger peer pressure becomes to force a sameness of behavior, ideas, and morals among those "individuals." Only a slavish conformity to the local individualist lifestyle qualifies one to belong to the local social group.

574. Re Glimmering #425. Another cosmic logical fallacy being committed today is the genetic error—the equation of personal origin of an idea with the truth or falsehood of it. In this cosmic version, the world is now concentrating on people and personalities, rather than on ideas. Voters elect personalities rather than platforms of ideas. We equate handsome with just, friendly with honest, charismatic with politically astute, and so on. If you like so and so, he must be all right for the job, or his theory must be correct, or his doctrine must be Biblical. Juries vote guilt or innocence depending upon their feeling for the prosecu-

tor or defense attorney. We must junk this emphasis. Truth, whether uttered by a handsome, well dressed gentleman, snarled by a fat old bag, or mumbled by a little kid, is still the truth, equally worthy in each case of belief. Return to a concentration on pure, undeceiving, unvarnished ideas; and leave the belief in personality to those who buy the offerings of advertisers.

575. What a great pity and a waste it is to die for the wrong idea.

576. The family is essential for raising children properly because only a father and a mother — not schools or child care centers — can teach their children the inner knowledge of humanity. Schools cannot transfer the whole cultural, intellectual, emotional, and spiritual content of the human heritage. Further, faith and tradition are viewed skeptically or negatively by the schools, and therefore will not be transferred to the students. Because institutions impart knowledge and values impersonally, they cannot create a commitment in the student to those values. Only a teacher who clearly believes what he is teaching has a chance to persuade his students.

577. I doubt that real objectivity can be found anywhere today. "Objective" teaching of religion and values now means "an unbeliever's view of a quaint old set of ideas, which a few people, somewhere, might still believe." "Objective" news reporting is absurdly slanted and even polemical; "objective" science, or literary criticism, or history is all prejudicially selected to demonstrate a preconceived point.

578. There is no such thing as an objective presentation of religion, just as there is no such thing as no religion.

579. As a major goal of their education, students must learn the difference between high sounding but empty statements and high sounding and meaningful statements.

580. Youth concentrates on the immediate in time and space, viewing what's close at hand as most valuable. This leads toward expediency. Age or maturity recognizes a larger perspective and sees value in the future, the past, and the distant, seeing theory or ideals as worthwhile causes for action. This is the foundation for moral and selfless behavior, as well as for large scale accomplishment.

581. Whether we should laugh because he is ridiculous or cry because he is pitiable.

582. He who trusts in the world and its goods knows neither this life nor the next. He is like an anesthetized ephemeris, destined to die the moment it wakes.

583. Twentieth century intellectualism is intellectually bankrupt, so most people almost instinctively avoid it or look down upon it. Intellectualism today, as promoted by the so-called liberals, amounts to little more than a squishy relativism which holds that all ideas are equally defensible. But if all ideas are equally defensible and if one idea is as good as another, then thinking, reasoning, and evaluating become unimportant, if not useless, activities. What kind of intellectualism is that? Further, these supposed modern intellectuals believe that truth is relative; but thinking—or intellectualization—is basically a process of associating absolutes.

584. I am not easily shocked by words or actions, not because I have seen everything (for indeed, I am experientially naive and innocent), but because I understand the possibilities of life: the capability of the unregulated human will, compelled by a hungry ego, the power of nature, the poverty of heart, the worship of self and of money.

585. As it ages, a ball point pen begins to leak. As it nears its end, the ink darkens. So with life.

586. "The Caldron suppled, what was grown too hard." — Herbert. Afflictions, rightly used, soften us and make us kinder. We must not let our sufferings harden us further, for then evil will beget evil, rather than good.

587. Before we learn *about* a text or philosophy we should learn the text or philosophy itself. One trouble with modern education is that we are always learning about something (through secondary sources) instead of learning the something itself (the primary works).

588. Art contains more truth about human nature than I had ever really imagined. Many of the verisimilitudes of art are actually profound and exact portraits of universal human characteristics.

589. The smallest things are the source of the greatest joy. Yes, there is satisfaction in big achievement, but don't you really find the most pleasure, happiness, and contentment when you get a hug, or find a parking meter with twenty minutes on it, or when your girlfriend or wife makes you a cup of tea, or when you get a nice letter, or see a hummingbird or a patch of wild grass, or when you find just what you want for less than you thought, or when someone agrees with your comment or idea, or when out of a whole symphony you hear just three or four notes that sound especially neat?

590. The smallest things are also responsible for some of our greatest annoyances and anxieties. How many people do you know—yourself, perhaps—who are upset by uncapped toothpaste tubes, elevator doors which close just as they are approached, a car in front going three miles per hour slower, a cup of coffee a sixteenth of an inch less filled than the one taken to another patron, the *other* line at the bank or store moving faster, and, of course, getting a teeny scratch on the car?

591. Since small things so largely determine our day to day happiness, we ought not overlook them. There exists a class of small things on the border between pleasures and irritants, and into which class each item in the border class falls is largely a matter of attitude. If you are determined to like or dislike something in this class—and sometimes this is true for larger things—you will. For example, if you just know you hate the smell of bleach, then bleach will smell hatefully bad to you. If on the other hand you determine at least to tolerate the smell if not to like it, by telling yourself, perhaps, that the smell signifies cleanliness, then you will be able to tolerate it. I associate the otherwise unpleasant smells of burning kerosene and of a tar and fish waterfront with happy childhood and memories of watching jets take off and of going to school near the ocean. If you don't like something, but cannot escape it, pretend it is something else, associate it with something nice, or view it as a positive symbol of something.

592. Why is it that every new scientific theory is held with tenacious and even vicious dogmatism, even though the scientists have seen one theory replace another at frequent intervals? The last to speak is always sure that he is right and has the final truth. Every age has laughed all previous ages to scorn and has felt self-approvingly content that it has finally been the age to have all the real answers and all the real truths. But the flimsy, prejudiced, narrow ideas of modern science, philosophy, psychology and so forth will be scornfully tossed into the trash by the next age, which will erect its own idiocies as the final revelation.

593. Sitting in front of the fire with a nice girl and a bowl of popcorn—how else can contentment be defined?

594. If you live long enough, you'll be able to be wrong about pretty nearly everything.

595. I hesitate to close doors and to write off possibilities, be-

cause often in the past when I have closed a door, God has reo-
pened it double wide, quite to my surprise. We cannot see
ahead, we cannot measure ultimate significance (or triviality),
we cannot place a percentage on the probability of an event. We
try to plan and we work toward specific goals, as we must and
should do, but we err the minute we begin to feel complacent or
make conclusionary assumptions.

596. Half our trouble is that we want to be *someone* great rather
than *something* great.

597. It is altogether a very serious matter when you take yourself seriously. Pedantry, pomposity, pride, ostentatious sophistication, snobbery — what idiocies do we put up with in the
names of education, civilization, and dignity. "What fools we
mortals be."

598. "Simplicity is the ultimate sophistication." — Computer ad-
vertisement. Our modern fear of being thought unintelligent or
unsophisticated has driven us toward an ever increasing complexity of language. The assumption that great, profound, or
even complex ideas must be difficult to comprehend or necessarily couched in obscure, twisted, lengthy sentences has result-
ed in the erection of verbal junk piles (yes, it is possible to erect
a junk pile) which have practically put an end to thought and
communication. The pretenders to sophistication gladly oblige
our desire for complexity on the surface by handing us layer
after layer of obscure language and long words and, especially,
many words. We get the proverbial reversal — the nut shell in an
Iliad, a brief comment spread over twenty five pages of prose, a
ten page statement diluted enough to fill a 300-page book. But
the computer ad's slogan is the real truth. The greatest profundities are expressed best in clear and simple language, which
allows the reader to look immediately beyond the language to
the thought. Proverbs and metaphors are the storehouses of
wisdom, not three volume treatises full of small type, big
words, and muddling sentiments. Only the blind and "un-

understanding" sneer at simple statements and call them simplistic.

599. If you turn the heat off, don't complain about the cold.

600. The most common fallacies of reasoning and thinking are those of hasty generalization and its converse, accident. Both of these arise from an uncritical extension of a fundamental human mind set: the assumption of continuity. We insist on and rely on and conclude from a continuity of perception and belief. We derive many of our anxieties from a fear of broken continuity, and many of our feelings of security from a guarantee of continuity (or at least from its assurance). Therefore, it is "only human" to extend a characteristic or event or phenomenon to cover a whole group or species—that is, to imagine a continuity of the observed characteristic throughout the group. (This method of reasoning and concluding is called induction.) But, too often the extension results in a logical fallacy because we cannot justly or correctly assume that continuity. Earthly life and human behavior lack consistency. Scarcely a greater folly exists than to attempt to predict behavior.

We drive along a rather smooth road and see a low spot with a stream running across. We assume that the stream has always been little and that the road underneath has been unaffected—is still smooth and hard like the road we can see. But in fact, the tempests of human life alter its waterways, and the roadbed beneath the water may be damaged, potholed, or even washed out.

601. How naive and categorical we are concerning human emotions. We speak of love and hate or honor and contempt as if they were at opposite poles. But no emotion necessarily excludes any other. One of my friends looks upon me with very great affection, and yet holds me essentially in contempt; believes that I have great potential, yet that I am hopelessly limited; says that I am superior to her in many specific ways, yet views me generally as inferior; and respects my ideas as good

but always disagrees with them in a way that implies they are beneath consideration. We often hear of a man who loves and hates his wife or girlfriend simultaneously and with equal vehemence. And many, many people are highly egotistical and yet have severe self doubts. Further, take those many events which inspire very mixed emotions, as for example, when an actress is turned down for a major role where a homely girl is needed, because the actress is too good looking.

602. Knowledge of certain loss can often be borne more easily than can an uncertainty of outcome. To be racked between hope and fear (or torn by indecision) creates more distress sometimes than the worst actuality.

603. True love is your wife letting you caress her even though you have band aids on your fingers.

604. For some of us, our great hunger for love, attention, and approval can leave us open to being duped by those who appear willing to satisfy us. We never question the sincerity of their motives, but rather we too readily and quickly extend and commit ourselves to them, and sacrifice for them, out of gratitude for their kindness. But when, as frequently happens, we are thus damaged emotionally by a false or temporary friend, we must avoid the bitter cynicism such events are likely to push us toward. For there are true friends, faithful loves, and disinterested praisers of ability. We must school ourselves to recognize them and support them in turn.

605. Reading too much what others say, without taking sufficient time to think about it, will ruin your mind. The powers of judgment, discrimination, and independent thinking diminish remarkably through lack of use, or never have opportunity to develop originally, if the brain is incessantly crammed with one external idea after another. Some of these ideas, still unexamined and unsifted, will become a part of your beliefs just by the workings of time. Constant influxes of information over a

long period of time, with no space allowed for reflection, can destroy all the higher faculties.

606. In their typically human action of ego saving and reconciling new information with previously conceived ideas, most people will nearly always believe themselves correct in their opinion of another, no matter what that other person does. If I, for example, have too hastily judged you as "too accepting of written opinions," and if you later prove that you really are not, I will not think, "I was wrong in my view of you," but rather, "Well, you have changed."

607. Each of us dreams of an ideal (or a hundred) which admittedly can be achieved by only one in a hundred million. Yet each of us also hopes—or worse, expects—that he shall be the one to achieve it. And yet there is a further yet, for by aiming at an ideal we shoot much farther than by aiming at the ground or across the valley. (This last idea is borrowed, but I can't find the source.)

608. People are like trees. Too much shade from larger ones hinders them; crowding stifles their growth; regular trimming makes them more fruitful, better shaped, and healthier; shaking by the wind strengthens their roots; outside food is necessary for best growth.

609. Prune your books, too; let the light through.

610. "For all of us have become like one who is over proud,
    And all our sophistications are like painted burlap,
    And all our weighty thoughts do evaporate like a swamp,
    And our egos, like giant blimps, have carried us away."
            —Isaiah 64:6 (Doax Version)

611. "I think; therefore, I believe." —motto of the intelligent Christian.

612. You can blow the spectacles off the old man in the last row of the uppermost balcony, but that does not prove that you've made music.

613. **Erroneous philosophies exalted today:**
    1. Selfishness — that you must always act only for yourself; always be self seeking; always ask, "What's in it for me?" not sacrifice for others; think of your own concerns first; call your own indulgences "fulfillment."
    2. Quantification — that all value lies in amount — that a thick book is more valuable than a thin book, which is more valuable than an article; that the dollar income of a person shows his human worth; that reading many books quickly is better than reading a few carefully; that something expensive must necessarily be better than something less expensive; that the more of an item sold, the better it must be (toothpaste, books, cars, philosophies).
    3. Individuation and Categorization of the world — that life can be divided into convenient, definable, and non-overlapping realms; that personal morality and political morality have no relationship; that opinions can be separated from facts in complicated issues.
    4. Expediency — that whatever works now, or is easiest, or cheapest, or takes off the pressure should be chosen, without regard to ideals, standards, or morals. If leaving the scene of an accident eliminates your problems, if betraying a weak ally gets you in better with someone more desirable or powerful, what's wrong with that?
    5. Modern Times and New Definitions have changed the nature of morality — that license is only freedom, that sexual promiscuity is normal and healthy, that legality is morality, that printed sex and hate and violence are freedom of the press.
    6. Intellectual anti-individualism — that all intelligent people have the same beliefs or at least fall into the same, few, definable camps; that certain ideas are acceptable and certain others are hatable and must be suppressed; that most things in science, philosophy, politics are defined, fixed, and agreed upon and

that therefore no dissent will be allowed; that a major lip service is that dissent should be allowed, but it really should be suppressed; that we must hate people who do not agree with us.

Re #3—that science, religion, art, history, philosophy, are different areas, which can be studied independently.

614. Let not my children come near a teacher who doesn't know the feel of dirt under his fingernails.

615. The ebbing and flowing bricks of wisdom cannot soar until they are strained through the concrete glass of fertile learned lumber embalmed in the pulse of those star-studded golden oceans of the speeding skyscrapers of knowledge.

616. We cry against needless complexity and ask for a pure and delightful simplicity, so they give us, "Beethoven's Ninth Symphony for Ukulele and Harmonica." We ask for dignity and power and instead of cowardice and weakness, so they give us, "Twinkle, Twinkle, Little Star for 132 piece orchestra, cathedral pipe organ, and artillery fire." Yes, you must have substance to start with. Package air and all you've got is a ping pong ball.

617. The Christian faith has nothing to fear from knowledge. The God who gave us our faith also created and ordered the world, so that no facts about the world will be contrary to faith. Men will, of course, interpret the meaning of facts as opposing faith, and other men will erect systems of facts to contradict faith, but time and disinterested thinking will show those interpretations and systems to be false.

618. It is easier to know facts than to know truth, for no thinking is required to know facts, only memory. Truth requires much thinking before it can be known, and thinking is hard. Thus, lazy as we are, most of us content ourselves with learning trifling but easy facts, and let others wrestle with truth.

619. There is at large in society, especially among those who as-

sociate themselves with the word "intellectual," a group of "anti-pinners down." These people object to all statements which are too clear, inclusive, definite, or exact, because all truths should be vague and indefinably complex. Thus, an anti-pinner down will always refer to a specific assertion as "unsatisfying," "unsatisfactory," "simplistic," "rigid," "limited" (in the negative connotation), or "facile" (again of negative connotation). Surely, we recognize the necessity of qualification and moderation in our thinking, but the anti-pinner down wants everything vague, weaseled, and open ended so that nothing too definite is asserted. Things have gotten so bad that someone who likes to be organized and specific is called a neurotic.

620. "'Impossible' is only an opinion."
"Okay, you fly a 747 around the world on a gallon of water."

621. One of the major problems with extensive experience is the Pavlov factor. The experienced man, who often thinks himself no fool, has long recognized the patterns of cause and effect in his line of work, and has perhaps thereby become a relatively competent diagnostician. But a strong tendency arises to rely completely on such previously learned categorized diagnoses, and our experienced man will often give up thinking altogether, in trade for instant association, in the same way that most people eventually begin to think in the clichés of their profession.

In his early days when he was willing to use his mind in the search for knowledge, our man would inquire into every fact and seek out every reason. When he found patterns, he was likely to conclude, for example, that "A is often one of the causes of B"; yet he continued to seek other possibilities. Now that he is the experienced man, however, and now that the delight of novelty has ceased, an entrenched boredom, a resistance to the new, and an overinflated sense of expertise have anesthetized his faculties. He has reduced his earlier conclusion to "A causes B."

As a beginner, he would read eagerly the literature of his

trade, thirstily drinking in every drop of information others were willing to supply. When he came across ideas he had no way of judging, he would graciously accept the consensus of the experts as provisionally true, and would regard those beliefs as wise distillations reduced from experience larger than his own, or from associations presently beyond his capacities. The assertions of fact were acceptable unless he should discover otherwise through his own experience. But now that he is the experienced man, he eschews with scorn all attempts to inform him, about things old or new. New publications he sees not as updates or refreshers or offerings of new material and procedures, but as impudent presumptions upon his supposed ignorance. He has certainly risen above his former teachers, and asserts that everything they taught him was wrong anyway. Such literature is for the green children of the business, not for the seasoned expert. His ways of doing things are better than those of the manual, because his ways are the old ways, are easier, and are apparently as workable.

The result of the Pavlov response by the experienced man, whether in a hospital, an automobile repair shop, or even in something like fire fighting or military strategy, is pandemic misdiagnosis. To draw the conclusion that "A is often one of the causes of B" took perhaps only a sixty percent occurrence of the A-B relationship. Now that the experienced man has relegated exceptions to a very minor position in his mind, his diagnosis in this case, for example, will be erroneous forty percent or more of the time. And if he reflexively treats A when present with B, and then pronounces a cure, he is very likely to have ignored either the real cause or contributing factors.

A further problem arises when changes come about through the revolutions of technology. Suppose that under new circumstances A no longer causes B, or that C is added to the causes of B. The experienced man is very hard to convince, *because* he is experienced, and his experience has never taught him these new facts.

We ought always be open to new ideas and be willing to give them fair hearing. Even the false ideas (which most new ones are, outside of technology) are helpful in clarifying our own conceptions and understandings of truth.

622. Give me a girl who is good natured, kind, agreeable, easy going, and affectionate—and you can keep beauty, money, body, even intelligence, though I give this last up reluctantly. But no, if the intelligent girl will hold me in subdued contempt (as so many seem to), will be contrary and disagreeable, cold and superior, always displeased and critical, then I choose the average-brains one. Give me the girl who will give me a hug, and you can keep the one who quotes Plato. I can look Plato up. This Glimmering is very nearly the opposite of my former opinion; perhaps I will change again someday. Or perhaps I had undervalued love before, because I thought it common and available.

623. Happiness is not the greatest good. To love God and to serve him is the greatest good. If this requires pain, unhappiness, and sacrifice then those things are involved in the greatest good. God does indeed want us to be happy, but given our own selfish and perverse natures, the fallen world, and the neurotic obsessions of the devil, happiness cannot always be guaranteed to us in this life.

624. He has been waiting so long that his bone china coffee cup had begun to rust.

625. "It was not just that he had never been loved by a woman, but that he missed it so severely, that had cast a perpetual shadow of melancholy over his soul." The same is true of everything we lack beyond the necessities—not having something pains not, until we desire it.

626. How dare we strive to triumph over others until we have triumphed over ourselves. And yet the most of men attempt triumphing over others rather than the self, because it is easier and more pleasing to conquer others, and because the ego is in-

flated thereby, instead of restrained, as when the self is conquered.

627. A painful, unrequited love is really a necessary part of the emotional education of every person because it teaches acceptance and it disciplines the heart. An unsuccessful lover also learns about the relationship between reason, passion, and will. Unsuccessful lovers have learned or acquired a greater maturity, understanding, kindness, and sometimes selflessness. Some people need this experience two or three or four times before their souls can be hammered into shape.

628. God sent his son to die on a cross rather than to conquer in battle because sacrifice is more difficult and shows a greater love. Conquest is a glorious act; sacrifice a humble one. Conquest is at least partly self rewarding, even when done for others, but sacrifice is selfless and completely other-oriented.

629. How often do we transfer our psychology onto others. We love or hate a person, and then not only do we assume the person reciprocates, but we interpret his statements and actions as expressions of the feelings we are looking for.

This is especially true of lovers, who don't see very clearly anyway. One in love will interpret a very cool statement from his beloved as a warm token of devotion and so on. And to those who hate, every neutral statement from the hate object is twisted mentally into an insult. This is all in our heads.

A further variety shows up among those skeptical people who don't believe anything possible they haven't personally experienced. Because something hasn't happened to them, they believe it cannot happen to anyone. Strangely, most of mankind is frighteningly bigoted, from the least educated or experienced, to the most. Humanities professors, who ought to be open to ideas, if anyone is to be, are horribly narrow, judging from my experience.

630. Melted down and cast away.

631. The nine tenths part of mankind seeks to elevate itself by censuring others. By attacking an equal or peer we would be thought better than he; this act is so common because we all find censure easier to produce than excellence. Also, in many cases our own state cannot be changed—so a woman, by attacking the beauty, virtue, or accomplishments of another, would seek to rise in the comparative balance. When we criticize, we try to imply our superiority, yet often succeed only in betraying our envy.

632. We try to claim or establish value and dignity for whatever we spend our time (or our whole lives) doing. Thus, even idle gossips may be found to have a system of rules and procedures for weighing and allowing—or rejecting—groundless scandals, and few people will be happy if told their method of making a living is useless, superfluous, idle, or even easy.

633. Once in a forest a naked young girl bathing in a stream discovered that a very old man had been watching her for a long time. "Why do you watch me bathe, old man?" she said. "Surely your age has placed you beyond carnal desires."

"You are right, fair creature," said the old man; "my quiet is no longer disturbed by my passions, but I can still be amazed by beauty. You have a house of exquisite construction for your soul. I pray that you will always keep it clean.

"My soul or my body?" asked the girl.

"Yes," answered the old man, apparently hearing imperfectly.

634. The speaker doesn't work, so we naturally blame the amplifier rather than the hook up wires—and of course we would never suspect the speaker. So when communication fails, we naturally blame the mind of the talker rather than the efficacy of his words—and of course we would never blame our own understandings.

635. What do you worship? Will your god bleed for you? Will the blood wash your soul?

636. Sweet peas will bloom in all their fragrance even while their roots feed in the leach line from a septic tank. But man's power for filtration and purification is not so great, and he is very likely to absorb some tincture from the material with which he feeds his mind. Therefore, when it is recommended that you read "good books," that adjective is well meant and significant.

637. How can any man be proud, when, if he understands events rightly, each day brings him new demonstrations of his incompetence?

638. How can you touch a rose and not worship God? Although ease of belief is certainly not a test of truth, yet if there is an Occam's razor of belief, it seems to me by far easier to believe that God made roses than to believe that they arose through chance and evolution.

639. Dead snails make no trails. — Proverb

640. How sad is the thirty-nine year old spinster who has sincerely believed that she was too good for each of her suitors, and who now wonders why a hero worthy of her has not yet arrived to beg her hand. She wonders how so many other women either find worthy men or else manage to stoop to marry men beneath themselves. She cannot understand how a man, unworthy when she knew him, now appears worthy in the arms of a woman who condescended to have him. Thus does our spinster not realize that our beliefs and preconceptions interfere with our perceptions. Her feelings of superiority prevent her from seeing the value in her suitors, nor does she realize that even the question of worthiness — a question many women never ask — creates a frigidity in her own heart and a criticality in her own attitude, which will be very hard ever to reconcile

with surrendering to a man.

641. "See the rose, vomiting its delicious aroma to the heavens."
— An image exactly defining modern art and aesthetics.

642. Having something, we undervalue it; not having something, we overvalue it.

643. "I know no disease of the soul, but ignorance; not of the
arts and sciences, but of itself." — Ben Jonson. It is one thing to
be blind, but quite another to be blind and yet believe you can
see.

644. Seeking glory for oneself is for people who have nothing
better to do.

645. When was the last time you talked to your soul, or asked
your heart what it was feeling (and why), or stepped back to see
whether your life was involved with truth and goodness or only
with idleness and vanity?

646. Remember the proverb, "It is not enough to speak, but to
speak true"? That formula could be applied to all of our intellectual endeavors, which must partake of truth or they are worse
than useless. Thus, "It is not enough to read, but to read true;
not enough to know, but to know true; not enough to believe,
but to believe true." This truth implies a continued scrutiny of
all that goes on both on the page and in our heads.

647. When, someday, you (or your plans) have been considered
and rejected, remember the greater pain of him who was rejected without being considered at all, because he was viewed as
beneath serious attention. And remember, when you come in
second, or third, or tenth, and the desire for victory and the disappointment have disturbed your heart — remember then the
contemplations of him who also had hoped to win, yet who
failed even to qualify for the race.

648. For them, knowing the standard answer, or the answer proposed by Freen and refuted by Spleen, is more important than knowing the real, true answer.

649. Ah foolish mortals! Forever blind to God's ways: too quickly confident and too quickly downcast; unable and unwilling to see the working of Providence in your lives, and always fighting God's will with an opposite extreme of hope or fear. What can I tell you? Trust God and be quiet.

650. A professor recently told me, "The book is already written; I just haven't put it down on paper yet." That kind of statement is perfectly acceptable in academia, where no one pays too much attention to reason, sense, or reality. However, suppose you go outside, and the man sitting on his back hoe drinking a beer tells you, "The hole is already dug; I just haven't taken out the dirt yet." Do you tell him to keep up the good work?

651. And at night the distant yowl of a lonely coyote, and the great silence of the stars.

652. People find pleasure and security in conformity. Thus we have best selling books and records, faddish fashions and activities, and polls taken after an election where we find that 85% of those asked voted for the winning candidate. That's not so bad, but when that psychology is applied to the conformity to popular ideas, it is very disturbing.

653. If you really want to help out the poor student, make your book shorter, print it in large type, and leave wide margins. Follow the old style: write clearly and concisely, and sum up each paragraph in the margin. Make your ideas live. Nobody likes to look at a dead body—even if it's the body of a most beautiful truth. And don't toss in a bunch of twenty-five-cent abstractions to prove how learned you are.

654. In praise of water. Wonderful water, versatile; sitting in fishponds, lakes, puddles, flowing in streams, rivers, pipes, ocean currents, the seas, tides, waves, foam, ice white with air or clear and solid, snowflakes, rain, hail, sleet, delicious cold ice water drinking, hot in showers and hot tubs and pools and coffee, and ice cubes for your tea, and washing your car, driveway, doggie, clothes, pour it in to temper wine, pump it through to manufacture paper, and everything from bologna to speaker cones, and don't forget to water your plants and grow your corn.

655. "Look at the price of this. Two dollars. It used to be one dollar."

"Well, they used to charge a dollar when a dollar was worth fifty cents. Now that it's worth only a quarter, they have to change two dollars."

656. Someone loves and marries the men who pump out septic tanks. And the vision of those women is clearer than ours, because they see and love the man, overlooking the necessary unpleasantness of his livelihood. We stick our noses in the air with a wrinkled face and exclaim, "No thanks, not for me. I'd rather marry a bank robber—he wouldn't come home dirty. We'll, maybe not a robber; maybe an atheist or even a professor, but a septic tank pumper? No way."

657. Your question asks for a long, deep drink at the Ganges, and how will I satisfy that with the squirt gun of my knowledge?

658. If, as we should, we bless God for a clean towel, how much more should we bless him for clean soul?

659. He spent his empty moments complaining about idle people who are always complaining about something.

660. The empirical method is useless for dealing with some

truths. How would you prove a man wrong who alleged that the second movement of Beethoven's Ninth Symphony is "a real toe tapper"?

661. A pencil and an egg are certainly not equal, but who is to say whether one is inferior to the other as an overall estimation. Darxul used to say, "It is difficult to write with an egg, whether hardboiled or raw," but then So-Fo used to say, "Chewing pencils is satisfying; swallowing them is not." To be different or unequal is not to be inferior. We each have gifts; let us use them.

662. I would rather marry a girl who came to me naked and bruised but who would pray on her knees with me, than I would marry a girl who came to me with ten million dollars and the vice presidency of her daddy's corporation but who was prideful and unbelieving. That may seem a silly preference, but it is mine.

663. The number of idle, lazy, copyist writers who steal their ideas from others rather than do their own thinking is lamentably large. The writer who reminded me of this added that too many authors simply accept the opinions they see in print, and, if the ideas are plausible, "pass them on without any further examination or thought."

664. People resist truth when they prefer to believe something else. — Proverb. You had forgotten, hadn't you?

665. As clean as you can get without being a bar of soap.

666. A small problem disturbs people more than a large one because small events are viewed as emblematic, while large ones are considered aberrations. Thus one spouse will grab the uncapped tube of toothpaste and yell, "This is what's wrong with our marriage. I want a divorce," while the same spouse easily forgave the other's crashing the new car.

667. "I love you."

"But I found out today from a friend that I'm obsessive compulsive and over rigid."

"I don't care what they call you or whether it has any relation to the truth about you. All I know is you—your personality and behavior and heart and soul, and I like them and I love you. So forget about the pigeon hole, whether you belong in it or not. I love you."

668. Sometimes it is better to make your own mistakes rather than to listen to other people and then make theirs.

669. We make a big mistake in expecting support and encouragement for our plans and ideas. The world delivers only attack, criticism and disapproval, by its nature; so expect opposition and ignore it. Indeed, be afraid if no one opposes you, for then your idea may really *not* be any good. All great ideas (and most idiotic and evil ideas) have been opposed and condemned, sometimes vociferously—or worse, have been ridiculed and laughed at. It is hard to be laughed at—I know it—but, Lord bless you, believe in your idea and seek God's help. Even if your scheme appears to be impossible now, or beyond your powers, try it. Once it was impossible for man to fly; now he has walked on the moon. Besides, though you may fail, you can still rejoice in the attempt, you can still learn from it, and you can still try again or perhaps try something else.

670. Lord God have mercy on a poor fool who strays even from his own crooked and winding ways.

671. You are just a pinch of tobacco, to be stuffed into a pipe; and when they have smoked it down and taken their pleasure, they scrape the dottle out onto the floor and tread it into the carpet. Or you are a Styrofoam coffee cup, useful and caressable, held and attended to, only as long as you continue to give pleasure. After the insides are used up, or when the flavor palls, you are crushed and trashed in a single unconcerned motion.

This is the age of more than disposable products—it is an age of disposable personal relationships, where people are used and abandoned in quantity. And the age has created its own morality to excuse and encourage the practice.

672. Pray not only for knowledge, but for an opportune memory.

673. A modern liberal is someone who buys a three gallon per minute shower head to conserve water and energy and then takes forty-five minute showers.

674. Do not get upset when you are contradicted. Your contradictor may be right. And if that uncertainty doesn't satisfy you, school your judgment and improve your knowledge so that you will usually be right; then you will be able to refute your contradictor, or at least not worry too much about him.

675. There are different kinds of discussion. In one kind, people hear views and exchange opinions and hear the arguments and reasons which led one person to a certain conclusion, all with the idea of understanding another's position and perhaps adjusting their own.

   In the more common kind of discussion, people simply air their prejudices in a hateful, rabid manner, and do not bother to do any thinking or take any external information into account. They don't listen for substance or ideas or reasons—they listen only for a pause, so that they might speak. Being persuaded by another is taken to be an admission of weakness and inferiority.

676. Those vague, high sounding phrases that let people sound important when they have nothing to say: indescri-babble. Half the world writes in indescri-babble.

677. No accurate judgment can be formed of an object by viewing it only from a single angle, and the same is true with many events. (That's how magicians can get away with so much.) So

too, knowing about something from only one perspective, source, or side will not allow a real knowledge.

678. I've always wanted a lime tree and a pet skunk.

679. You can paint a dirty eave and make it look clean for awhile; but the dirt is there underneath, and it will slough off the paint pretty soon. Hear this, O man. First clean your eaves, and then your paint will stick. Indeed, clean your eaves well enough and you may not need paint.

680. The word "tool" is often used in a derogatory way, as, "He's a tool of the commies," or "He's a capitalist tool." The expression is derogatory because a tool is passive and obedient to the will of the mechanic. But I don't know that that is reason for condemnation. A tool is really very important. Having the right tool is often essential to the performance of some task, and it always makes the procedure easier and faster. Anyone who has tried to loosen a nut with his fingers, drive a nail with his fist, or tighten a screw with his fingernail recognizes this. We never see a mechanic run into the shop in the morning and yell with contempt, "You are all tools of the establishment!" Put a man bare handed in a field and he will pluck a few weeds; give him a wrench and he will build a power plant to light and heat the homes of a million people.

681. "The door to this classroom is farther down the hall, sir," said the student.

"Silence, peasant. I know this campus perfectly well," answered the professor as he turned abruptly around and walked into the wall. As he held his bleeding nose, he was heart to mutter, "Now why did they move the door?" Darxul, hearing of this, said, "Pride never doubteth, even when his nose bleedeth." Be humble. Humility makes it easier for you to recognize your mistakes in action and your errors of belief. The proud man walks confidently off a cliff.

687. Those who think little and write much tend, in a given age, to overwhelm the world with their products and to have their names trumpeted in the world as if they had something to say or knew something worthy. This is the usual mistaken equation between quantity and quality — one of the major curses of the modern era. Moreover, the quantity writers push aside the works of those who think much and write little (and often bless the world with a gift of culture or wisdom) because the public always falls for the *ad populum* argument ("just everybody's buying this guy") and for the big name. So *Porn in the Cornfield* becomes a bestseller because Joe Famous wrote it (supposedly) and because it was promoted.

688. Justice requires consistency.

689. A "good day" is not one because you have been happy or avoided frustration, but because you have served God.

690. A. "I think my mind is going downhill."
  B. "Mine's going uphill right now."
  C. "Well, mine's just coasting along."
  D. "I think mine's stopped."

691. When we fill a salt shaker, we take care not to spill even a few grains, though they have essentially no value at all. Yet we seldom take care to be kind, helpful, or thankful; we don't work very hard to create or preserve happy moments.
  "Did you serve me in compassion and faith while on earth?"
  "No, but at least I never spilt any salt when I filled the shaker."

692. Every bolt should have a nut, but there should be a lock washer to hold them together. Hence, wedding rings.

693. Do not labor only for distinction. The man who places third in the International Champagne Drink Off has distinction, and

even a trophy. Rather, labor to be a good human being.

694. What a disappointment to be a disappointment to God.

695. We all say at one time or another that we will turn over a new leaf, but we find too soon that the leaf is made of concrete several inches thick and is well settled in the ground by force of habit. Turning it over is much harder than we thought, and sometimes all we can do is lift it a little before it drops back into place.

696. People attack skunks for only one attribute—the creature's very effective defense mechanism. Yet the skunk who prowls around our house runs when we open the door, is a delight to watch because of his unique dancing walk, and is a real help to us by eating earwigs and other bugs. He's also beautiful. If this isn't the description of a hero, what is?

697. A Beethoven symphony—or any exquisite piece of music which bears frequent hearing—is like an old friend. A bizarre or poor interpretation is like your friend when he is drunk—still your friend, but my goodness. . . .

698. One of the hardest things about life to be admitted is that most of us most of the time get just exactly what we deserve.

699. Two basic orientations account for the outlook and behavior of most people, and define the underlying motivations of their actions. These are the "give orientation" and the "take orientation." The takers are openly selfish, believing that that leads to or creates happiness; yet they are likewise almost bitter in their dissatisfaction with life because they are profoundly unhappy. Such is the necessary result of selfishness. But the takers believe the problem to be one of not enough selfishness, so they are continually becoming more and more grasping, expedient, and self-oriented. Our society has been pushing in the direction of the take orientation for the past ten years, and thus we see

increasing unhappiness and disaffection.

700. A cherished object of hate. People love to hate—perhaps even need to hate.

701. When logic advances, fear backs off.

702. Not everything real can be seen.

703. Many people seem to have a deep-seated need to hate and to be angry. Our sinful natures find hate very satisfying, but genuine occasions or objects really deserving to be hated do not occur often enough to satisfy us. So we find targets for our hatred—either slight things inflated out of proportion, or things made out to be evil or hatable, like Hitler's Jews. We like to hate without reason or proof, because proof is often lacking or not sufficient to justify the degree of hatred we feel, because reason usually argues against emotional hatred. When we hate or are angry, we feel superior; thus, hatred and anger are really based in pride to some extent. See *Rambler* 11.

704. Love not arising from understanding is passion, not love.

705. Every Christian should be humble, but none should be passive in the face of an evil world. We must indeed "surrender" to Christ, but then we must join his army and begin to fight again—this time on his side.

706. Heaven is a community property state. A wife who supports and helps and encourages her husband shares his reward.

707. Fragile words tentatively offered from uncertain lips may yet contain more solid and violent truth than the boldest assertions of sneering confidence. We must stop being the victims of fancy packaging.

708. How can we ever know what another person is really like?

When we first meet someone, we make all kinds of hasty generalizations based on just a short conversation—this person is
very philosophical, that one has a melancholy temperament,
that one has no morals. From then on, everything we hear about
that person and everything else the person says must fit into
our generalization, and we twist and filter the information (un-
consciously, unless we are careful to make sure we don't) to fit.
Further, as that person becomes our friend, he will tend to fill
the role we expect of him. People fill role expectations for several reasons. Roles are comfortable; people desire to please; some
people have a self-uncertainty; others enjoy the opportunity to
be several different people and yet be consistent to any one
friend; some yield to the expectations or the psychological pressure put upon them. Only after a long acquaintance can you
discover what a person is really like, unless you take pains to
reduce your prejudices and demands and let the person be himself. The bungler, milktoast, wit, hero, or boring person may not
really be like that at all if you could once allow him to be himself. Also, of course, in love relationships, people put on their
best behavior and thus try to impress each other by deceit. In
these cases the "best" way to find out the truth is to marry the
person. However, the consequences are usually pretty bad.

A problem arises from this latter case. If deceit leads to misery, shouldn't you be honest in love? Yes, certainly. But then
one takes the risk that he will never be loved or married, because those who put on the act appear much more attractive.
The consolation is that if you do marry after being your honest
self, you will have a much better chance of being happy.

709. You can't be a grape all your life; everybody turns into a
raisin eventually. But the grape which has cultivated its sugars
will make a sweet raisin.

710. We spend quite a lot of time thinking about tomorrow, and
about some goal two or three years off. And such thinking and
planning is good—even essential—in regulating our lives. But
two periods in our lives that we usually neglect need at least as

much attention: to assure that we can steer straight through tomorrow and through that near goal, we ought to keep one eye on today (that it may not be ignored, spent idly, or used in pursuing a wrong direction) and one eye upon twenty years from now (that we may be able to see in some perspective the value of our current efforts and the true significance of our hopes and fears.

711. He is a weak man indeed who fears the laugh of fools, and, compared to God, who is wise?

712. It is true that the devil is holding the world hostage, but I have never seen a more willing bunch of victims.

713. Approach your problems the way a weight lifter approaches his weights: silent and determined beforehand, he does not brag, nor does he cower. Then at the moment of attempt he concentrates his whole body and soul into a kind of directed violence which will allow no uncertainty, no hesitation, no half-heartedness.

714. What thoughts do you have when you first see your spouse after being apart all day? What thoughts do you suppose your spouse has? What would you like your spouse to think, and how can you live to make those thoughts real?

715. Now move to the realm of supreme importance. What thoughts do you have when first you come to God each day? What do you suppose God thinks of you? What would you have him think of you? And how can you live to make those thoughts real?

716. The reign of the self is the reign of inhumanity.

717. There is no tale so amazing, bizarre, or incredible as a true tale. We foolishly require of our fiction that events be probable and believable, that characters be human and consistent, and

that some connection with reason and motivation be maintained throughout. But real life operates under none of these constraints, and a story such as we would fling away with a sneer of disgust, if found in a novel, is the common occurrence of every day.

And if we accustom ourselves to regulate our lives and our expectations by the behavior we find in books, we will be not merely disappointed, but horrified by the conviction that we are acting alone, that most people are unacquainted with the simple and logical motivations ascribed to them, and that most people act through the stimulus of what, were it not so common, might be called a kind of mania. Perhaps it is cliché to remember the complexity of the human heart; yet few appear to recognize the significance of that complexity. Even a person long trained and greatly experienced in introspection often has difficulty in adequately discovering his reasons, motivations, desires, and fears involved in the simplest interhuman transaction.

718. Of the "journalistic six," the questions Who? What? When? Where? and How? all deal with relative simplicity. But the last question—Why?—leaves the mere chain of events behind and enters the regions of philosophy and the human heart, or even the divine will. It of all questions is the most difficult to answer fully and correctly, if indeed it can be answered at all. It is the most important question, and the most rarely asked.

719. A thousand clear, explicit, and irrefutable demonstrations will be found still inconclusive by him who desires to believe otherwise. For the heart, especially when inflated by pride or self interest or love, will not be overmatched by the reason; some "yet" or "even so" will always be found to grab onto. Not only do our beliefs constantly recommend themselves to us (because they are familiar and because they are ours, and because we have settled them into our overall intellectual network), but our desire to continue to believe them works so strongly in us that it bends, alters, or even creates our perceptions of things. Diogenes said, "The easiest thing of all is to deceive oneself, for

what a man wishes he generally believes to be true."

720. What epitaph do you want on your tombstone?

721. **Love. A Poem.**
Acceptance. Entire, open-hearted welcoming. Not "putting up with" some things, or viewing some trait of personality with a secret disgust. But always mentally embracing that other — from phobias to pimples.

Compassion. Never feeling contempt or scorn for any sincere human being striving for virtue and truth, or for one who would strive if he could, or knew how. Sympathizing with pains and distresses, though you cannot feel or even understand them, and being disturbed until you can alleviate them.

Selflessness. Turning aside from self-interest and being willing to give without hope or desire of return. Sacrificing because you know someone else needs it. A humble, generous desire to give of yourself and to do good things because good things ought to be done, not because you expect gratitude.

Understanding. A gentle and unsuperior tolerance of a soul different from yours, yet with cares and concerns, hopes and fears, desires and expectations equally powerful with yours, and felt with equal or greater pain or joy.

Caring. An almost instinctive concern for the welfare and happiness of a being, made in the image of God, especially placed in your life or under your protection, to be valued and cherished more than your eyes, more than the breath of your body, more than your favorite folly.

Encouragement. A willing and active support. Adding your light to extend the vision, and your hand to assure the steps. Praising little victories, knowing that all great conquests come from them. Changing the orientation of the entire world by saying, simply, "You're right, and I'm with you."

Forgiveness. Letting go of wrongs, forgetting hurts, holding no grudges. The freshness of forgiveness erasing past offenses. Welcoming the forgiven into open, unconditionally loving arms, and making all things new.

Kindness. A warm focus on the needs of another, helping with a friendly gentleness, with happy generosity, and with unassuming grace.

722. Faults are corrected in another not by pointing them out but by demonstrating to him the corresponding virtue. If he is selfish, demonstrate selflessness to him.

723. He was seldom original but his sayings were always true.

724. We must not only *have* ideas; we must *use* them. One of the basic tenets of the *Rambler*.

725. **A Prayer for the Morning**.
Bless me in this day, O Lord, that I might honor you, and that I may do something to serve and to please you. Help me to reflect the image of Christ in my words and actions, and show me how I can help other people with their needs. Enable me to bear both the real evils and the petty frustrations which will be brought upon me, or which I will bring upon myself; give me courage and strength that I may not become disheartened in the face of opposition or defeat; and prevent me from indulging idleness, selfishness, or folly. Bless all who love you, and grant us your protection and guidance. In Jesus' name, Amen.

726. Carrel E25. A little boxed-in cubicle separating us from everything human and natural. Such is modern civilization. We isolate ourselves from each other so we can pursue a detached, narrow train of thought broken off from all context.

727. Lord, it distresses me to find that great service is not easy, and that perhaps it is not even in my powers. I want to reach up and grasp a star, but all I can do is stumble over the rocks in the path before me.

728. If an exposé of the antics of human pride weren't so sad or so personally applicable, we would all laugh loudly.

682. How easy it is to fill one's head with wrong ideas — they abound everywhere, and many of them are attractive, irresistible almost. How difficult to rid oneself of wrong ideas, what sad and reluctant parting, what struggle inside. How still much more difficult to obtain correct ideas, worthy, true, and good. No one champions them with the enthusiasm and vociferousness given to the bad.

683. Why do we always refuse to admit that a price must be paid for everything — that every act or freedom or lifestyle or choice involves necessarily associated problems and difficulties?

684. A truly moral man thinks about values both abstractly and in various possible applications, before he needs them as a protector for himself or others. But most people do not think about values until a crisis arises through a lack of morality. A man wants others to be moral around him — as for himself or for others in affairs not concerning him, he doesn't care. The man who sees a car pull in front of him at a gas pump or who has his groceries stolen from the back seat suddenly wants honesty in the world — when he shoplifted the tobacco or shortchanged the station attendant, he cared not for morals. A moral system cannot be invoked at will — it must be pervasively established and omnipresent or it will be useless. Suppose a man flies into a cloud in his private airplane and then watches his gyro horizon break. At that moment he many certainly think, "Someone ought to do something about quality," but that thought won't help him recover from a spin.

685. When you first see an earwig — or a thousand — it strikes you as a horrid and disgusting creature. But after encountering millions of them day after day, you can watch one almost with interest as he dinks along the cement, his twin pincer tails in the air and his antennae waving.

686. Murder and divorce arise essentially from selfishness. Train your children not to be selfish.

729. When Darxul parted from anyone, he commonly offered this benediction: "May all your hatreds turn to love, and may all your loves be reciprocated."

730. To a hundred billion grains of sand underfoot we are indifferent; to one grain in the eye we are very attentive.

731. What unhappiness to know that what you want most does not even exist.

732. Home is wherever there is a good book, a cup of hot tea, and someone who loves you.

733. The Clean Up the Government League went bankrupt trying to pay the soap bills.

734. Some when they marry are thinking of balance sheets; others are thinking of bed sheets.

735. **A Prayer.**
Lord God, when the bee stings, and when the night comes, and when the wind blows, give me the patience and strength to endure what I cannot change, and turn those evils from which I cannot yet be delivered to the repair of my soul and the improvement of my heart.
Remind me that you love me, and remind me also that wounds heal, the wind is stilled, and the day returns.
And may your will be done in all the things, for Jesus' sake, Amen.

736. The Golden Rule includes the truth that other people are human beings, too, and are entitled to the same respect, compassion, mercy, and love which we want others to pay to us.

737. How vain to desire others to think well of us, yet to be valued by others is one of the most fundamental of human needs.

And if our desire for others to admire us implies that we will work to deserve their admiration, then perhaps it is all right.

738. The vanity and selfishness of men's goals, the blindness of pursuit, the narrowness of their values, and their puny and limited considerations mislead them into believing that the highest value is whatever they desire immediately. The supreme value in the world is not success, happiness, victory, power, wealth, patriotism, length of life—not even life itself—not single mindedness or loyalty to a personal, corporate, social or national goal. It is righteousness—to love and to serve God in truth. The praisers of expediency forget righteousness and abstracted justice in order to praise an act of extreme and inhuman cruelty because it works and it proves the "dedication" of the torturers. Such a philosophy is sick.

739. Only the simple is universal.

740. Almost no one allows others, the world, or its events to present themselves as they are—to be what they really are in fact. Each person at some remote period has established a collection of opinions and attitudes—mostly arbitrary, and mostly derived from emotional responses rather than reasoned conclusions—to which everything he perceives must be fitted agreeably. For any situation there are narrowly defined limitations to what we will allow to be true. Everything is twisted, quite automatically, to harmonize with prejudices, preconceptions, or extant opinions; if it can't be, it is rejected as impossible, incredible, or false. The process occurs so automatically that almost nothing we perceive (or think we perceive) is real—we only imagine it to be so. Why do we falsify the truth? Partly from habit (we are accustomed to finding square blocks in our toy chest), partly from our need for consistency (we like to stack all the uniform blocks in even rows), and partly from pride in our opinion (we have always known all the blocks in the world must be square like the ones we have touched). How hard this process makes the discovery or recognition of truth, especially

considering that men are no friends to truth, anyway. And how hard it is for man to learn, or to realize (and admit) he has been wrong.

741. Feel pity and compassion as God feels them; not with a touch of contempt and superiority, but empathetically, with tenderness and understanding and a desire to help.

742. "Cheer up, God loves you and wants to help you, and I work for God. What can I do for you?"

743. Our worldly society is like the world — spinning in circles. It rotates about the self. Only the society dizzies itself into insensibility, and the centrifugal force throws off humanity, values, spiritual concerns, and leaves only the airy, fluffy dross too light to move. The pure metal of mankind has been tapped off unseen while the floating slag has been exalted for the name of the metal it used to contain.

744. While some scars on the human soul exist which must, perhaps, strictly be called indelible, yet with love and care they can be erased to such a faintness and can have such new and beautiful lines drawn over them, that almost no evidence of deformity will remain. An understanding love is the best therapy for heart and soul — the emotional and psychological problems of the most troubled can be healed best by it.

745. The world examines the faith with a pair of tweezers and a glove, and expects to make a correct judgment about its texture.

746. Some people refuse to be happy. They will not be pleased with anything; they criticize everything. They let petty and meaningless things disturb their quiet days, inflating bad out of proportion and discounting good. They feed their hate and resentment, putting everything negative in the strongest terms, and twisting everything against themselves. They get a whim in the head that so and so should have called but didn't, and soon

this non act has been amplified into, "Why does so and so hate me so much? What have I done? And why must I be persecuted?" Or the box they got some item in is dented and soon this is, "Those crooked clerks are always trying to shove their defective merchandise off on me. I'm going back to demand an exchange. Oh, life is so hard when everyone conspires against you." Johnson said some people think it's a proof of delicacy when they refuse to be pleased. They don't have better taste or higher standards, just more pride. Quality and even perfection are important goals, but in trivial things mass produced or areas where quality or perfection is seldom met with, to make it a prerequisite for happiness is ridiculous. To grow heated with resentment because your hamburger was ill assembled only makes life more difficult. Patiently reassemble it or tell yourself, "It's good enough for me, " or both. When you make your own hamburger, be perfect. The next time you meet one of these oh-look-someone-has-opened-his-door-against-my-car-and-knocked-some-of-the-paint-off-if-I-knew-who-did-it-I'd-punch-him-in-the-eye-and-break-out-his-windshield-and-now-I'm-so-upset-I-can't-enjoy-the-movie type persons, just say, "Oh be quiet. It's still good enough for you, even with a little scratch on it."

747. "A woman needs a man like a fish needs a bicycle," the women's libbers like to say, and at first this may sound clever and witty even though untrue. But when one realizes the unspeakable human misery—the great and profound unhappiness of soul—upon which that statement is built, it is not very amusing at all. God made man and woman for each other, not just for mutual help and friendship, but for marriage—a lifelong unification of work, worship, and goals, the great and true mystery of two becoming one, combining different perspectives and ideas and souls so that the whole of life might be lived. Moreover, permanent heterosexual love is the radical principle of terrestrial happiness, and it cannot be circumvented or substituted for.

748. We are an illiterate society because we never allow our

children to read real books. When a child is ten, he should be reading standard classics. When he begins to read at three or four, he should have something worthwhile—something with an *idea* in it—not the "Jane saw Spot barf" type of book. The pride of adults makes them look down on children, who could learn and read and think amazingly well if given the chance. Why shouldn't a child learn to read any sentence he can comprehend verbally? McGuffey's readers are "too hard" nowadays not because our children have become jelly brains, but because we have.

749. Wake up you idiot. This is a bad world. This is the real world. You're upset because your order didn't arrive or because your zipper broke or because someone slighted you. Would you rather have been raped, or have watched your child die under the wheels of a truck? Or maybe you'd prefer to starve to death in Cambodia. Count your blessings, idle one, and do not invent irritations. You have it too well in life already; bless God and pray that being cut off in traffic is the worst that shall ever befall you.

750. If we were honest with ourselves and others, and if we paid attention to the world around us—especially the natural world—we would spend much of our time in tearful awe, or even stunned with amazement. How wondrous—or awful, in its original sense—is the first motion of an infant, the flow of water, the destructive beauty of fire, the bending of a blade of grass in the wind. But wonder implies ignorance or submission to powerful forces we cannot comprehend, so we pretend not to be impressed or surprised or awed by anything. Nothing is new to us; we've seen it all and done it all; there's nothing special or amazing about anything; after all we're modern and sophisticated. We act this way not because of our knowledge, but because of our pride.

751. **A quadramental idea**:
    1. We listen very attentively to our own opinions in the

mouths of others.

2. The man who finally persuades us is the one who tells us what we wish to believe.

3. When another's opinion is the same as ours, we consider the matter proved beyond all doubt. If his opinion differs, well, what conclusion can be drawn from the ranting bigotries of the ignorant and stupid?

4. We notice (without vanity, of course) that the most intelligent and clear thinking and wise people always share our opinions (though, curiously, sometimes a person is very intelligent on some matters and very stupid on others—but then this is true even when we *don't* use a ruler printed on a rubber band).

A Corollary to the QM idea: We may not always be reasonable or have the facts straight, or understand the issues or really know what we're talking about, but at least we are always right.

752. When someone tells us how wonderfully intelligent and perceptive we are in detecting false flatterers, we humbly promote him and marry him to our daughter.

753. There is no such thing as neutrality, for neutrality moves by gravity and the wind in the direction of evil. Not to resist evil is to yield to it; to permit it is to support it. To do nothing is to do harm because of the degenerative nature of the world.

754. Johnson says that a Christian "will be willing to impart his knowledge without fearing lest he should impair his own importance by the improvement of his hearer" (Sermon 11). Pride and the desire to retain power prevent many "experts" from teaching very much because they fear revealing their "secrets" which give them their distinction and superiority. I had one teacher, an air conditioner repairman turned instructor, who spoke only in general terms and never demonstrated anything specific about real world fixes. He was evidently afraid we would replace him. But our value as human beings does not lie in the uniqueness of our knowledge any more than it does in the amount of our wealth.

755. Not what you read here makes you a better man, but what you read afterwards in your heart, and what you do afterwards in your life.

756. Most people do not need to be delivered from circumstances; they need to be delivered from themselves.

757. If you choose the right books, you need not read many to grow wise. But you can read an industrial furnace full of today's intellectual sawdust manufactured for bulk consumption without adding anything other than falsehoods and distortions to your mind's supply.

758. Every second that our eyes are open, the existence around us demands an explanation for its very being and a decision about its purpose and meaning. And what explanation does man give? He looks upon a butterfly, or a walking stick, or a spider in his web, or a Venus fly trap or a rose bud, and he says, "This is the meaningless product of a meaningless chain of meaningless accidents." Then man humbly names his species *homo sapiens* — "wise man."

759. All things — from stereo music volume to Biblical interpretation to wickedness of heart and action — will continue to move in the direction of their original corrupting impetus, toward excess and enormity, if unopposed or unchecked. Virtue doesn't do this because it bogs down in an alien world. And sometimes virtue just gets tired.

760. Most people think so seldom and so little that when they finally sit down to try to think something through, they drive themselves into hysteria and panic because they equate imagination with thought and possibility with probability.

761. Do not be downcast by the scoffers who inform you, in a tone of triumph and condescension, that the success of your

scheme will not rid the world of evil, since there are many bad things in the world and your scheme addresses only one. No one can perform every task, and no one is called to. The barn has to be shoveled out one scoop at a time. The scoffers sit back and pretend to see a whole and the diminutiveness of your effort by comparison, but they themselves do nothing about anything, so what is the measure of their effort?

762. People have an inner need to complain, even pout a little bit, about minor things—hurts or desires or disappointments—because of the attention, concern, and sympathy it gets them, and the relief it offers to life's otherwise unameliorable frustrations. Everyone needs someone to listen sympathetically to his complaints. Remember as a child how mommy's concern made you feel valued? We all need to be valued and attended to, even when we have no obvious external wants.

763. Every time you plan to do something, ask yourself first, "Is this act reasonable? Am I behaving rationally? Is this well thought out and purposeful? Have I considered this action calmly and thoughtfully?" By doing this you will soon become indecisive, inactive, and insane.

764. People grow increasingly selfish in a desperate attempt to obtain happiness. They reason thusly in their disappointment: "If selfishness doesn't work, what I need is a whole lot more selfishness." Thus they become utterly selfish and utterly miserable.

765. As the man who spoke backwards used to say, "It is not an unbad idea."

766. There is light enough for those who wish to follow the path, and darkness enough for those who wish to hide along the wayside.

767. "I'm sorry he tromped mud in all over your rug, but he's

retarded, you know, and he never thinks of his feet." And what excuse does a man use who never thinks of his soul?

768. "Are you still driving last year's old fashioned truth? Just wait till you see this year's new improved truth."

769. Never rigidly define or categorize a person; you may be wrong, and even if you are right, he may change. Do not rely on first, or second, or third impressions for your understanding another's personality. Keep your perceptions open and study the person over a good period of time under differing circumstances. No wonder so many people complain they have "married a stranger": they formed a half baked notion of the person at the first meeting, and then required all that person's acts from then on to conform to that impression. First impressions have little value, first, because people are complex. And second, at any given moment when we might meet a person, he is harassed by fifty transient follies, oppressed by ten short-lived troubles, or enamored by some new but passing pet scheme, or just distracted somewhat by his current business or pleasure.

Once I had dinner with a woman soon after I had read Joshua Reynolds' *Discourses on Art*. The work was fresh in my mind, and as often happens in such cases two or three of his points seemed pertinent to whatever we were discussing. I was told at the end of the evening that Reynolds must be a really big thing in my life, since I had grounded all my philosophy on him. Until you can discriminate accurately between a person's permanent philosophy (that is, the one which remains basically the same and is subject only to refinements) and his current but fortuitous and distorted mind set, do not let yourself believe you know him.

770. Why read literature and philosophy? To assemble ten notions of one concept? To collect possibilities? No, but to decide—to believe and to reject—and to act. Books should help you think better, live better, serve God better; you must interact with them to find truth and value, and they will make you hap-

pier, more creative, more understanding of yourself, the world, and human nature. Hence, you will grow confident and compassionate by banning fear and bigotry. Literary criticism today is generally only a technique for identifying meaning or for tracing associations. Since it never judges—is this idea good or true?—it is essentially sterile—nay, dead.

771. Reason in man is weak and fallen, but we ought not therefore ignore, reject, and abandon it. Reason can be trained and strengthened, and be of good service.

772. How often we reach a conclusion and sit back in our chair to think self-benevolent thoughts, when five minutes later we learn that we did not even have the correct premises.

773. How often we believe we are finished when we had only inadvertently pulled the straw away from the bottom of the glass.

774. "Give a man a fish and he will have a meal; teach him how to fish and he will have many meals." —Proverb
    Explain the meaning of a verse to a man and he will understand that verse; teach him how to interpret, and he will understand many verses.

[January, 1980; age 29]

775. We seldom thank and praise God for the failure of our plan, but many times we should.

776. Moral truth cannot be examined or tested by the rules and procedures of science, nor is it neutral as the scientific method purports to be. Yet moral truth possesses infinitely greater value than scientific truth because what affects the soul eternally is immeasurably more important than what affects a transitory body.

777. Our scientific mindset encourages us to isolate and categorize and objectify and plasticize everything into a rigid and unchangeable item, as if separate and independent from everything else. But as I have said before, everything interrelates, and does so in a flexible way, always changing that relationship.

778. We spend a lot of our time trying to enact what we have imagined. How necessary then to have a regulated imagination. A good plan *may* have a bizarre result, but a bizarre plan can scarcely have anything else.

779. Look down from an airplane upon a crowded football stadium, where you can see in perspective the vanity and idleness of human attention and effort, the useless intensity, and think how earnest and proud they are of their endeavors.

780. The key to understanding any civilization can be found in how it regards women sexually. Indeed, the quality of our whole belief in the meaning of human existence is tied to and can be traced from our sexual attitudes toward women. Crucial here also is the potential split between enunciated values and real practice, and the resulting possibility of a theoretically civilized nation moving into barbarity.

Every man needs a woman's body to play with and enjoy, and vice versa—that is the way we are made. But in the truest civilization, sex is a spiritual and an intellectual act as well as an emotional and physical one, an act of such closeness, unity, and meaning that it and its implications require a rather exalted notion of the process and the woman involved (as a spiritual and intellectual being). Sex is not just two bodies coming together, but two people coming together through the medium of their bodies. It is an intensely private and personal communication and affirmation. That's why we are so self-conscious and careful about it. The animals just copulate without any thought or concern beyond their instincts. But we are much more than animals.

As sex in a society begins to grow less than the ideal, as it moves from all inclusive to emotional to physical to mechanical, the society itself will move that way, and its other values will show it. As women move toward being viewed as mere objects, objects of passing pleasure, art moves toward mere decoration or surface paint, thought moves from profundity to frivolity, issues become both oversimplified and impossible to comprehend, love becomes a superficial impulse without commitment, the universe becomes a mere collection of meaningless particles, man sees himself and the cosmos in a continually reduced way, and all meaning becomes an accidental or vestigial attachment to a brute impulse to copulate. If woman is a mere object to photograph and use and beat on when you are mad at her, what then are you?

The Bible teaches the doctrine of sexual fidelity because of the profound sexual significance of women, and not only because of the possibilities of pregnancy or venereal disease or psychological and emotional harm. When a society begins to teach or to institute a community of women (as Marx and modern morality teach), its culture and civilization dissolve, and its values, purpose, and happiness decline. The implications for religion are quite clear, which is why Samuel Johnson once wrote that "religion and marriage have the same enemies."

781. Look down from an airplane upon a nudist camp, where every creature is separated from his external trappings. Watch them play volleyball or lie in the sun, and then you will see that human pride is the most amazing of all phenomena.

782. If you tell Mrs. Henrietta Tishley that you really like her mink coat and matching leather purse and shoes, she will be pleased. But if you tell her you really like her outer wrap of strangled animal pelts and the use of the skin of the same dead cow to make her purse and shoes, she will not be pleased. You see, things don't matter to people as much as how the things are perceived or what is believed about them.

783. Many people believe in the mental fabrication of neutrality

or non-commitment as a convenient and guiltless way to escape acting upon their principles—or as a convenient and guiltless way to avoid having principles.

784. A government of ignorant and vain men corrupted by their own power can neither judge wisely nor legislate justly.

785. Everyone needs to have some successes, however tiny or seemingly insignificant, in order to maintain sanity, self respect, and happiness. The need for accomplishment is basic to human nature. Constant failure and frustration create hatred, fear, misery, depression, despair, and eventually insanity. Some highly frustrated persons resort to obsessive behavior such as repeatedly putting a nut on a bolt or assembling and disassembling something, to manufacture successes, even though rather mechanically and arbitrarily. Women sometimes bake cookies when they are frustrated; men work on the car; both sometimes combat frustration by buying things. Love therefore should reveal itself in the praise of little successes, like the great job your spouse or friend did in finding an address or sewing on a button, because the small successes will help to offset the small failures, and maybe even the large ones. Few people praise others because few people love others, and success tends to incite envy rather than admiration in our proud and selfish hearts.

786. Our first desire is to be accepted; our second is to be superior.

787. We impose our affectations on others and then must impose the credulity on ourselves that others will believe them real.

788. We must pity the self-conscious individual, for even though his fear of failure and anxiety results from a prideful concern about what people will think, we cannot ravage and devastate his ego by telling him that no one truly cares what he says or does. How falsely he believes that every word will be

marked, recorded, remembered, judged, and that his entire reputation (as if that mattered) will depend forever upon his next
words. But do we soothe his fears by telling him of his utter insignificance, or of the truth that no man is much regarded by
others? No, he probably thinks little enough of himself in spite
of his pitiful pride.

789. "Yes, they are shackles, but they are made of gold." Ah, the
heart of man.

790. Some expect—almost require—a manifestation of the Holy
Spirit to result in wild, emotional behavior, physical paroxysms,
and probably speaking in tongues. But the Spirit does not act
the same all the time. Sometimes he speaks very softly; sometimes he can be heard only in the echo of a teardrop.

791. "All my plans failed; my life is ruined. I wish I were dead."
No, my child. Your life is not ruined. It will be different from
the one you would have had if your plans had succeeded, but
not necessarily worse. It may even be better. Do not allow a
gnawing regret of the past to be an excuse for future laziness.
What you need now are new plans, not tears.

792. Our universities are training students to react rather than to
think. And it is a mechanical reaction, patterned after the predictable events of a chemical experiment in a test tube. Like
computerized number crunching, the thinking process is as-
sumed to be fact crunching, where the correct quantity and loca-
tion of circumscribed events will necessarily lead to a correct
solution. (This assumption is invoked in order to avoid the
"problem" of values and morals.) But thinking is a human endeavor, based, to be sure, upon certain established rules of reasoning, but not really adaptable to the rigidity of a+b=c. I certainly believe in and teach the use of the syllogism, the inductive and deductive processes, and the avoidance of specific material fallacies; but there is an unquantifiable finesse to good
quality thinking. There is a *quality* factor involved in the prem-

ises of one's argument—premises whose accuracy, scope, truth, clarity, distinctions, and so on can vary infinitely. Sodium chloride and distilled water don't have these difficulties in the lab. And there is a *judgment* factor involved in examining fallacies — or any argument—and judgment can be a product only of wide reading, deep thinking, accurately comprehended experience, and frequent discussion with those known for good judgment.

Real thinking, if taught or permitted on campus, would lead to much diversity of opinion and to conclusions undesired by the faculty. The university is not the free marketplace of ideas it would like others to believe it is—or that it tells itself it is. Thinking is very dangerous, whether done correctly or fallaciously.

Thinking also differs from scientific method in that our principal instrument, the mind, is subject to illusion and delusion. We sometimes half willingly misperceive those events and concepts from which we form premises.

793. We always have the soil under our feet, to remind us that death and decay are real, and that we are mortal.

794. Darxul, wise and old, known for his equanimity in the face of difficulty, once said, "Behold my sons, I give you one of the golden keys of life: learn early how to accept frustration without disordering your soul. 'In this world you will have tribulation'; the events of our existence here are so ordered that man will be frustrated in most of the desires of his heart and in many of his endeavors. Yet to react with anxiety or passion, to allow the mind to stagnate or the heart to petrify, brings neither cure nor benefit. Cease from complaints, and make humble supplication to God that when the ground slips from beneath one foot as you climb up the slope of existence, your other foot may find a firmer hold."

795. One day Darxul sat upon the rock in front of his house and said, "Many stoics are well known for their perseverance and equanimity in the face of tranquility. Words of philosophy are

useful in proportion as they are true; but even when they possess truth itself, they cannot often heal the heart. Truth is a comfort to the mind; only time and love can heal the heart."

796. One morning Darxul came out of his house later than usual and said to his waiting students: "You know that I am human; therefore, you will not be surprised that I, too, am sometimes lazy. Today's truths I will read from *The Book of One Hundred Truths*." These are the ones he read:

1. The truth will make you free, but many are interested in neither truth nor freedom. Truth is too painful and freedom too fearful to accept.

2. Few believe what they desire to be false.

3. Among the living, fame arises from publicity rather than from excellence.

4. Do not ask what others do; ask what it is right to do.

5. A lemon may be called an orange, but it must still be a lemon.

6. The law may say, "Yes," when righteousness says, "No," for the law is in the hands of men and righteousness belongs to God.

7. *What seems* and *what is* differ often.

8. A man can be known by what he seeks.

797. The strength of the *ad populum* fallacy and the weakness of independent reason are continually demonstrated from childhood to old age. We see children everywhere constantly turning in expectation to their parents after the occurrence of some event or the discovery of some object, with the question on their faces, "What is our reaction to this? Is it frightening or is it funny? Is this a disaster or a success?" Older children will sometimes ask, "We're having fun, aren't we?" or even, "Am I happy?" As we grow toward adulthood we begin to have our own feelings and judgments, but they are still tentative and insecure, so we ask each other, "This is good, isn't it?"

To learn "how the eagerness of one raises eagerness in another," how we are "seduced by example and inflamed by competition," do as Samuel Johnson suggests in *Idler* 56 and visit an auction. Then reflect how whole lives are auctioned off by those who fall in love on the basis of popularity or the number of admirers of the opposite sex. Though because we are human we will always need approval, we really ought to learn to think for ourselves and to make decisions without requiring their validation by others. And we ought to form our self image on something other than the whimsical, biased, and hastily generalized opinion of some other person.

798. The rightness of a doctrine remains unaltered regardless of its misinterpretation or misapplication.

799. "Come to me, all of you who are tired and loaded down with your work, and I will give you rest. Put on my yoke and I will teach you to plow, for I am gentle and humble of heart, and from me you shall find rest for your souls. For my yoke is comfortable and my burden is light." —Matthew 11:28-30 (Doax Version)

800. The great continuum of human life shows at one end a flight from moral responsibility, and at the other a pursuit of riches or pleasure or general hedonism. This is the whole momentum of our existence. Who can wonder then that the truth of the Christian faith will be resisted with all the heat and violence men can muster, because the faith teaches, "*You are guilty,*" and "The pursuit of riches and pleasure is vain and foolish"? Christianity crashes against our selfish, fleeing hearts, our fallen nature, our whole being as it exists in ourselves and in a society apart from God.

801. When we deal with human nature, no such maxim exists as one "too obvious to be stated." Most truths we forget because we find it convenient to forget them. It might seem too obvious to need stating that judgments should follow and derive from the reasons or premises upon which they are based. But men generally form a judgment or opinion first and then seek rea-

sons afterwards.

802. A thing, idea, or person perfectly good in itself—excellent and fulfilling, proper and useful, kind and intelligent—will very often be scorned and rejected by him who compares it with something once believed or perceived to be superior. The concept, "I have already rejected better, and so cannot now accept an inferior"—even though that supposed better exists only in memory or imagination or is not now obtainable—enslaves the mind and prevents many happinesses. Pride puts the chains on the will, and even if the will could break through and accept the "perfectly good," pride would gnaw away at the soul, taunting him who chose less than he once could have had and destroying his peace.

Pride can thus make you a prisoner of your past whenever it controls you adversely—when you turn down a good job because once you had or were offered better, or turn away a lover because you have already rejected someone you think was superior, or refuse to be content or happy with any performance or thing (from ice cream to symphonies to roses to architecture) unless it equals or surpasses what you experienced in the past. It may be a worthwhile labor to seek the perfect reading of Beethoven's 9th Symphony (meaning one which most closely matches your own taste and style and judgment), but to sneer with disgust at every version which fails to match your favorite so far would make unhappy and unenjoyable what ought to be a delightful endeavor. Again, in your own performances always work to improve and to do the best you can—the drive to excel and the slight dissatisfaction with less than a best effort are healthy, until they begin to oppress you and destroy your happiness and quiet and productivity.

The next question, of course, is, How do you conquer pride? Happiness is so much a product of psychological orientation, and dependent on expectation and allowable perception (what your mind will allow you to perceive) that it cannot be obtained by the will, or by mere events or possessions. The heart must be freed from pride before happiness can enter.

803. To the news media, everything has become an "incident." Rape, murder, mayhem, invasions of other countries, traffic tickets, all are just incidents. Two things bother me about this. One is that the word carries just a slight tinge of implication that what happened was a minor occurrence, all over now, so you folks are safe from it, so don't worry, just enjoy the hideous details. The second thing is that the word implies that the event can be separated from the rest of reality and can be examined dispassionately as something that—surprise—just sort of happened, and has no significance or implications for our society. A four year old child was brutally murdered yesterday, but this little incident occurred across town, and besides, your kids are all grown, so you need not worry or think. Oh, it happened next door and you have a daughter the same age? Well, then, this incident must be more surprising. But incidents happen, you know. Don't you watch the news? Maybe you'd better watch to see if any little incident happens to you.

804. Do not thoughtlessly seek the "best obtainable" or the "best you can afford." Give some consideration to use, to technological supplantation, and to need.

805. How do we measure the worth of a human being? (And should we even say that one human being is more valuable than another? That would depend upon "valuable" in what way—to employer, society, God.) Human worth cannot be measured by money—that is a perpetual error of our greedy hearts. Is a person making $30,000 a year twice the human being as one making $15,000? Or when Mr. $15,000 gets a raise to $20,000, has he become one third better? Nor can we measure worth by IQ or even by creativity—for while people blessed with large amounts of either or both of these frequently help to improve living standards, and (at least in the past) culture, that is merely their calling, and they cannot be said to contribute to human happiness or the service of God in a way fundamentally worthier than someone who cooks or plants trees, or sympathizes, or

holds the hand of a child while he learns to walk.

We are required to perform to the full extent of our abilities and to use the talents we have been given. If human worth can be measured, then, it must depend first on the attainment of what is necessary, rather than what is luxurious, and secondly on what the human must attain voluntarily and through work. And I would focus on the area which is the most difficult of all to measure—the capacity to love, to be kind, to be compassionate. Since God, and not we, reads hearts, perhaps we should leave all valuation up to him, and consider all men of equal value.

806. "The people desire falsehood in their hearts," thought Darxul. "It is the very comfort of their wickedness." But in order to warn the innocent, the old man read from *The Book of One Hundred Lies*:

1. You can trust me.
2. I'll love you just as much in the morning as I do tonight. (Or, "Of course I'll still respect you in the morning.")
3. I'm doing this for your own good.
4. The check is in the mail.
5. Don't worry; it's only a game.
6. I'm from the government and I'm here to help you.
7. This hurts me more than it hurts you.
8. If you agree this time, I'll never ask you again. Just this once.
9. That cannot happen.
10. I promise not to tell anyone.
11. Lies! Lies! All lies!
12. I'll repay you just as soon as I can.
13. Buy this and you will be happy.

807. The vanity mirror is the only rightly named product. We should also have vanity car, vanity stereo, vanity house, vanity boyfriend, vanity mink coat, even vanity values and ideas— those kind that show up in everyone's mouth, even among those who brush regularly. How can you prove that you're

tuned in to the times unless your mind becomes a pop station, complete with boom box, reverb amp and disco programming?

808. We spend much of our lives pretending to be something we are not rather than trying to *become* something we are not. Pretending is easier; we are not really convinced that the thing we pretend to be is really what we want to be; we pretend to be different things to different people, and we could never become all those things. We are actors all, but how do we tell which is our character and which is us? Whom do we see in the mirror at midnight, alone with us in the bathroom? If I'm putting on a philosophical act for you (or for my ego) then I swindled you, and you ought to trash this.

809. We believe some very great lies, however obviously false and proved so by our own experience, simply because we want them to be true. Example: You can take without giving. Try it; you'll be ruined. And you'll be up to your elbows in the lacerated hearts of all your friends.

810. Rest for the soul comes in the midst of work.

811. I am very disturbed by the growing supplantation of moral reasons for action by selfish reasons. We should improve health conditions in the garment industry not from our moral duty as humans to other humans, not from compassion or even a cold sense of rightness, but, the television tells us because the mouse droppings get all over the clothes you buy and therefore you are involved. That's like saying, we ought to put a rail up around this drop forge because when the workers fall into it, their blood gets all over the forgings and our customers won't like that. Another real example. We must not let the Russians enslave the whole Middle East, not because we believe in freedom and oppose imperialism or communism, or war, or killing, but because we won't get any oil if we let them take over. And when the Russians invaded Afghanistan, we didn't dare say they had done an immoral act, or that justice required us to cut off their

grain purchases. No, we said they were wrong and our cut off was "patriotic."

812. Having failed to discover either the origin or destiny of the universe, and being convinced it has no meaning, the materialists look at a rock, a pond, a fish, and each other, and then happily conclude that they understand the world.

813. What wonders could the schools, the magazines, newspapers, and television achieve if they would labor for quality. People take what you give them, as long as it's popular, whether it works ultimately for their improvement or their destruction. Whatever you give them, they take, adjust to, and come to expect more. The only problem point is that thinking is harder than feeling. Oh, people could be given wisdom, culture, knowledge, and take it and be happy with it; but in ratings and circulation battles, someone will always go for the gut, and once that happens it's all downhill. Lower and lower standards of quality take over as mere titillation and spectacle become normative, and violence and sex and banality reign. Certain people, in advertising, government, politics, and business, don't mind the drop at all. They know that when people think emotionally instead of rationally they can be persuaded (indoctrinated) to buy or believe what the clever psychologist wants them to.

814. "What's the matter?"
        "Oh, nothing. It's just that I've failed as a human being."
        "Do you know anyone who has succeeded?"
        "Well, I've failed worse than anybody else."
        "And are you satisfied enough with that to leave it at that and always look back on it, or do you want to become a 'successful human being'—whatever that is?"
        "But I'll always be a failure and won't become a success."
        "Lazy, huh?"
        "No, but I just can't. I was born to fail, or something."
        "I see you enjoy the security of failure. Not much risk in that, is there?"

"I hate being a failure; I just can't help it."

"Well, all I can say is that you'll be rewarded for trying and not punished for failing. I know it hurts to fail. My only advice must overlook that. And it's this: Grit your teeth and try till your guts fall out. And may God bless you with success by doing his will."

815. As much as I favor reducing the pride of mankind and instilling a just humility in every heart, even I feel concern for the maintenance of a certain amount of human dignity when I walk into a bathroom at a convention hall and see on opposite walls twin fourteen foot long stainless steel troughs functioning as communal urinals. Certainly there can be no vanity or possessiveness in wishing for a few moments of privacy while answering the call of nature.

816. After observing the frenzy of the world, Darxul added these to *The Book of One Hundred Lies*:

14. New is better. (And new is true; old is false.)
15. New is worse.
16. Change is progress.
17. Change is never progress.
18. Wealth is happiness.

817. Pride sustains an enormous capacity in the human heart for hatred and resentment. Some say humans have a need to hate, just as they need to love. (The very wicked, even, afraid to love another human being, have a pet animal as the object of their love.) Hatred often lasts longer and is more intense than love, because true love is a humble emotion, giving oneself up to and for another, while hatred is an emotion of pride, making one feel superior.

818. One afternoon he came home early. "Bad judgment has left me penniless and out of favor," he told his wife. "The project failed and now both my power and money are gone. Tomorrow the papers will call me a ludicrous and disreputable schemer,

and the stores will visit the court to attach our house and cars. If therefore your love for me was contingent upon money, power, success, or a good name, you must consider now what you will do."

819. How often, in reading or thinking, we come suddenly to some new realization and then exclaim, "What an idiot I have been—I've been completely wrong, but now I understand. At last I've achieved the wisdom and growth and maturity I only thought I had before. All things seem so clear now—how could I not have seen this before?" And indeed we have been blessed with a new portion of enlightenment. Our only mistake is in thinking it is the last. A lifetime of struggle and seeking and revelations must pass before we can really understand anything much. And the profoundest truths, about God, the incarnation, and so forth, can never be perfectly understood. But then again, if we create a category called "The Perfectly Understood," where shall a man find a thing to put into it?

820. The news makes sure that everything happening is bad— even the weather. "No relief from this heat; the same drab weather will continue; it's raining now and more bad weather is coming."

821. If you can keep the sneer of superiority off of your face and the phony boost of self congratulation out of your heart, spend a day sitting around some public promenade observing peo- ple—not in order to criticize them or exercise your contempt, but to learn about and to understand humanity. See if you can detect their orientation toward themselves, others, life. Watch their faces, their walk, gestures; listen to what they say as they pass. Contemplate the happy and the sad, the serious and the frivolous, and the indifferent. What are they pursuing in life? What is on the throne in their hearts? Do you see how many of them have no other real deficiency than love?

822. Maxims are really of very little use except as reminders or

as starting points for one's own thoughts. It is good to read over them often and to think about them, but by themselves they will not teach you. "It is not right to do evil that good may come" helps us in our thinking as a touchstone of action, but it cannot be fully understood or known except after prolonged experience of the world. Seek to understand the classic sententia in the context of application.

823. After consulting his own records and the recommendations and cautions of several prestigious books and magazines, and after a prolonged period of agonizing over his final selection, the connoisseur opened a bottle of fifty year old wine, only to be disheartened to find it still three years too young. His day ruined, he could only sit in his study and sulk.

824. We really ought to stop valuing everything by comparison and popularity. Too often rare things are valued *only* because rare, with little or no regard either to use or ornament. An ugly, canceled postage stamp is more sought after than a beautiful new one just because it is more rare and because it is sought after by others. If this foolishness stopped with stamps, it would perhaps deserve no notice, but we humans desire, attend to and value almost everything—even other people—only because others desire them, pay attention to them, or value them. We also create rarity merely to increase value—only a certain number of art prints, designer clothes, or "collector's editions" are produced. And how often the phrase, "limited edition" is touted as if that makes something more worthwhile or desirable. Even more, we try to keep the standards as stringent as possible so not too many can get in. For example, probably eighty percent of all women are pretty good looking, but we allow only a very few to be called "beautiful" because beauty ought to be rare; so by strict comparison we eliminate many who in another setting would be quite lovely. Drop into practically any fast food restaurant and see how many really cute girls there are in the world. We ignore them only because we don't want to glut the market, in the same way the large diamond mines hold off

their inventories to keep prices up.

825. One day a man saw a lovely and precious orchid in a hot house, and immediately it became the desire of his heart. He wanted that orchid terribly and painfully, but he could not have it. In his agony he sometimes felt resentment toward the flower, but he really knew that his hurt was of his own making, and that the orchid had no guilt either in its existence, or in its beauty, or in its unavailability.

826. We mistakenly value our performance for the day by measuring the time we spend "working." We often say, "I put in a good day—twelve hours of correcting papers (or filling orders or auditing the books or calculating stress or checking specifications or welding pipes or serving food)." Then on a lazy day off when we have spent the time musing and occasionally thinking, we say regretfully, "What a wasted day. All I did was to learn that I have undervalued many things because they were familiar, common, or easily available; and to realize that pride is my enemy."

827. "He is never deceived who never trusts" (Proverb)—and he who never trusts never lives.

828. A person you meet infrequently will be imperfectly understood by too little contact, and will therefore take the form and personality you create for him through the unconscious exercise of extended imagination, and the psychological phenomena of "gap filling" (making up supposedly harmonious or consistent facts to complete a partial picture) and generalizing.

829. Someone has said we like what we read because we find ourselves there. On this basis, here are instructions on how to be a philosopher, wise man, or utterer of brilliant sayings. First, leave lots of details out and supply generalizations so the reader can fill in the blanks with his own imaginings; next, be vague so that he can interpret your statement after his own heart, and

therefore think he agrees with you. A lot of thoughts apparently true, profound, or extensively applicable are, upon close scrutiny, discovered to be merely vague. I'm not talking only about those thirty-two-page gold leafed presentation books (like the ones decliningly middle-aged non reading women give to each other), all filled (one to a page) with statements that seem to mean something deep if only one could tell what—sayings like, "Reach out and touch love, and the stars will come closer" (having just made that up, I kind of like it).

I refer to books of "really purportedly real" ideas, with pretensions to truth and profundity at least equal to those of this wonderful book. Yet I do not mean to criticize them very much, and I would even praise them some, because the very lack of excessive specificity leaves room for the imagination and the understanding to work to make the statement clear and real in a personally applicable way. If a saying makes you think and leads you somewhere, it is okay. The best philosophy like the best poetry and painting, must leave room for the imagination and the thought to work. Suggesting is as important as telling. But art that is so diffuse as to suggest nothing (except that you are wasting your time or that the artist is a fine con man), like maxims or philosophy that is so vague as to say nothing at all, should be avoided or at least not exalted to the skies.

830. If we would be led by the light of truth, we must open our eyes to see it.

831. The audiophile tossed and turned half the night, agonizing over his system, thinking about every component, distracted by a vague dissatisfaction. Finally he dozed off, but awoke suddenly at 4:30 and yelled, "I hate my phono cartridge. That's the entire problem with my life."

832. If you walk through life briskly with your head down, you will never know where you are going or where you have been. Pause in your journey occasionally and look around; you may not even be on the right trail. Don't get caught up in the one-

foot-in-front-of-the-other syndrome.

833. "I failed."

But you can't say you haven't learned something. You still weren't right, but as least you were wrong in a new way. Men usually find truth by exhausting all the possibilities of error. The only short ways to truth are chance, which favors few; and belief, which the pride of man prevents or obstructs. He must find truth his own way — the way of pain and disappointment — by testing all the specious, false possibilities, and then at length and somewhat unwillingly, accepting the only remaining answer.

"But I have failed."

Yes, but you have also succeeded in learning that something doesn't work, and so you know some truth you didn't know before. Thus, every failure is also a success.

"But, you lousy semanticist, it still hurts."

Yes, and I cannot do anything about that, except sympathize. It is the human condition.

834. **Psychology**.

"There's Harold over there. What do you think?"

"I dunno. He's okay, I guess."

"*Okay?* He drives a Mercedes 450 SLC and lives in Newport."

"Well, he *is* pretty good looking."

"And he's a vice president in charge of something at a computer company."

"He seems like a really nice guy. You wanna introduce us?"

"Ah, he already has girls all over the place."

"Now I want to meet him more than ever. I think I'm falling in love."

835. Some people are evil because their hearts are evil; some are evil only because they see others being evil and are led to imitate them.

836. "I don't know what I want, but I sure want it bad."

837. "We love the truth as long as it lets us do what we want."

838. Every ordinary person—that is, everyone lacking the constant flattering attention paid to beauty, wealth, or power, or lacking a large and self sustaining ego even in the face of contrary information—almost every one of us, in other words, suspects or even firmly believes at one time or another that he is a reject on the assembly line of life, the one balloon with a hole in it out of the whole box, the soap that leaves the bathtub ring, the leaky milk carton that everybody pushes aside to get at the good ones, the toy with the inferior batteries that go dead first, the Brand X in the supermarket of existence.

Our pride, of course, exaggerates the rejection and intensifies the hurt, but at bottom the rejection is real, because that is the condition and practice of humanity. The rarity of love, especially compared to the great amounts of envy, pride, and selfishness, makes men cruel and anti-compassionate. A human being is no longer seen as inherently valuable or even potentially improvable. People are now just like disposable cans—get what you can from them and then throw them away. Indeed, if someone today tells you that you have potential, as often as not that is a statement of rejection—"Yes you can improve but I want nothing to do with it, you inferior creep. I prefer someone who is already perfect." Ah dear, how many people are genuinely surprised to discover that the person they marry is only human after all. And then they compound that folly by feeling resentment and disgust and anger. Ah, man.

839. We see a candle and believe it to be a bonfire—for who wants to admit that knows only a little?

840. Human nature is not so varied or so difficult to understand as it first seems. It is complex, all right, but the real block is that people find it difficult to understand because they refuse to recognize and accept the paradoxical quality of life—that a person

can want and not want the same thing at the same time, that he can both desire and fear something, love and hate, be generous and selfish in one act, be humble and proud, hate himself and be egotistical. Pascal calls man "the glory and the scum of the world," and he could well be speaking of one man. To understand human nature we must also recognize that people are generally afraid of truth, that they prefer a life of illusion or self delusion — and they will hate you if you deliver them — and that common sense operates only superficially and intermittently, because most of the time people act unreasonably. Further they often act without any motive at all; sometimes they refuse to act even in the face of overwhelming motivation; sometimes they go against their desires for no reason, or for such a reason as being afraid to do what seems so clear and obvious. We all spend our time raising insignificance to essentiality and in reducing importance to triviality.

John and Jane at the breakfast table do not exchange words of support or affection, or discuss how better to raise their children or live in the world or serve God; they argue about who put the spots on the mirror in the bathroom, and who is responsible and guilty and wicked for the little dent in the car. Yes, man has reason, but he also has passions, pride, selfishness, and immaturity, and often he does not want to understand or be kind.

And we speak to each other in code, hoping to get messages across which we are afraid to say directly. When a wife tells her husband, "I want a new sofa," it may mean, "Our sex life is not adequate." Think of all the coded buzz words in letters of recommendation. "This student is energetic, punctual, likable, and open to suggestion," means "This poor, stupid, plodding, unimaginative kid needs all the help he can get, for with a mind like his, he's going nowhere." Or "Miss Blank is intelligent, personable, and attractive," means "I hope she sells soon, because this dummy is going nowhere by herself."

841. Because every beginning creates a movement or action which if continued will yield some result, whether success or

failure (which will then suggest a redirection or reevaluation), it is possible to reach the truth even though beginning with false premises. The road is long, though, and somewhere along the way the false premises must be denied, abandoned, or misinterpreted, at least implicitly. Some people believe, because of their own pride, that their false premises led them to success, and the accomplished fact of success serves them as a powerful argument, though of course to realize the effect you intended doesn't mean you have caused it, and even when you did cause it, you may not have done so through the means you believe. In theory it is always sunny; in practice it rains. Do not forget to figure in the rust factor.

842. Is the sadness in the heart of a gnat less than that in the heart of an elephant?

843. "My word is as good as my check," said the forger as he handed over a partial payment and promised to pay the balance later.

844. Punch and Judy hold their clubs in their arms because they have no hands, not because arms are better than hands. Never confuse necessity with choice, and beware of the practice of ignorant imitation.

845. A strand of spaghetti, no matter how carefully made and how perfect a specimen from the finest ingredients, will still be unable to pry a nail out of the wall. The best and the worst spaghetti strands you can find or produce will be equally useless for the performance of a task impertinent or alien to the function for which they were designed, if that function requires qualities different from those of an ideal specimen. Cross application (an old thing used in a new way) is a wonderful means of enhancing utility (you *can* use a very strong screwdriver to pry a nail out of a wall though a weak screwdriver would bend), but we ought to be careful about so often insisting that an item will perform function B just because it is superior (not ordinary)

in design or performance for function A. This is the doctrine of pertinent quality.

846 Text: Mark 3:5-6. Strange behavior, you say. But it is quintessentially human, coming from proud and hard hearts. The Pharisees were seized with fear and envy. In human nature the direction of envy is not to emulate the envied person, but to destroy him. And their fear arose from believing that their power was being threatened. Envy and power conflicts are two of the worst propagators of evil and unhappiness in the world.

847. Submitting to direction or advice consciously reduces the extent of your choices, free will, and independence, and therefore irritates the proud heart. But allowing yourself to be manipulated, whether subconsciously or more or less obviously, allows you to preserve an illusion of independence, choice, and self reliance. Appeals to your reason, to your judgment, to your sense of trust in a friend you will hear none of; and yet you blame advertisers and politicians and arguers of all kinds for using emotional appeals, reverse psychology, hidden suggestions, and all kinds of logical fallacies. These are what you respond to—how can you then say you do not like them?

848. When asked what he thought of the angry and impassioned speech he had just heard, Darxul opened *The Book of One Hundred Lies* and read:
    19. Equality means sameness.
    20. Selfishness creates happiness.

849. Umber stood philosophically on the prow of the ship, deeply inhaling the fresh sea air, feeling the warmth of the bright sunshine on his face, and ignoring, or perhaps not hearing, the burst of the whip as it lacerated the backs of the struggling slaves in the galley. But in the midst of enjoying his view, he felt a particle of dust fly into his eye. He blinked and rubbed a bit, and got it out, but his eye was reddened and irritated. "Well," he said stoically, "life has many pains, and we must learn to

bear them as best we can." He then called upon his servants and his friends to sympathize with his suffering, and found some satisfaction in complaining of his hurt.

850. The instruments and controls in the cockpit of an airplane appear confusing and incomprehensible, impossible for anyone to use or understand; but this seems so only because you are trying to look at everything at once and take in the whole continually. Do what the pilot does: look at one instrument at a time, and you will see how clear and easy the instrument panel becomes. Any large accomplishment will seem difficult or impossible if viewed as a single task of incalculable proportions; but when you realize that it can (and must be) broken down into a series of small tasks, then it becomes rather easy to perform. See *Rambler* 137.

851. When an event concludes differently from our wishes, we call it a failure, though often in reality we have only incorrectly defined success.

852. "Mouthful, little flavor; small bite, great flavor." — Chinese proverb.

853. People resist the Holy Spirit not because Christianity is doctrinally or rationally difficult to believe, and only partly because they resent its interference with an immoral lifestyle. The real objection is that the faith requires humility and submission — displacing the self as the pivot of individual existence. And just as the pride of human hearts prevents so many terrestrial happinesses, it stands against spiritual fulfillment and salvation with all the strength its grabby tightfistedness can exert. How do we view humility? Oh, we praise it abstractly, but we secretly despise it. "He was certainly humbled," we say with superiority and contempt. "How humiliating!" we shout with rage as if we were entitled to some exalted state above that which we have just been shown as our own. Do you ever hear anyone say, "Thank God I was humbled yesterday?" Do you

ever say it? No, we look in the mirror and say, "There he is folks, the world famous super champion, better than anyone else in every way. He doesn't need anyone's help." We don't say, "Who will teach me something today?" but, "What pitiful human will I condescend to endure today while he tells me something that's either obvious or completely wrong?"

854. A few philosophers and many people believe that the name of a thing is rooted in its essence and descriptive of the real nature of the thing—that the exact, unique, and fixed name of a thing necessarily derives from it, rather than being only a convenient label or symbol more or less arbitrarily attached by man. Words and names easily divert attention, perception, and belief from essences, because man yields to externals in almost every situation. The Sklud Toothpaste Company recognizes that no one would buy its product if named after the company, even if the toothpaste were the best on the market. So it calls its product "Angel Brite" and people buy it even though it is rather mediocre. Similarly, since the name *is* the thing for so many people, a real estate developer will offer you some property at Pleasant Meadows, without mentioning that he has renamed it from Rat Bone Gulch, by which term the area was known for over a hundred years. Look, too, at the prejudices about people's names. Who will allow a Herman to have a dynamic and exciting personality? Who will allow a Gertrude to be beautiful?

855. War, as terrible and barbaric as it has always been, has in recent years become completely uncivilized. Soldiers have always committed atrocities on civilians, but those were always accounted deplorable, accidental, and outside the limits of "ideal" warfare, just as terrorist acts, like blowing up buses and planes, have been condemned. Formerly the morality of war limited the killing to members of the rival armies. But since World War II when both sides began to destroy civilian populations, atrocities have become a standard part of military strategy, whether by being bombed in an attempt at demoralization or by being murdered for helping the enemy (as have been sev-

eral village populations in Viet Nam, Afghanistan, and Africa). Part of this may be attributed to the blurring of civilian versus military, where civilians operated factories in their homes in Germany and Japan or where village civilians took up arms as non-uniformed soldiers in Viet Nam (though in the latter case, it has always been considered murder to kill even a soldier in uniform when he was unarmed).

"Winning" a war—that is, to force the other side to surrender on your terms—involves two goals: first, to destroy the ability of the opponent to fight, and second, to destroy his will to fight (for if the will remains, he will recoup his ability and fight again). Further, if the will to fight is destroyed, even though technical ability remains, a surrender can be achieved early. Thus, this latter goal is admirable, because it can end a war sooner than working out the complete destruction of one army's equipment and manpower. That's why propaganda plays an important military role. "Give up; you don't have a chance," if ever effective, could save lives. However, to achieve an admirable goal through evil means is a Machiavellian step neither side ever should have taken.

And now, with nuclear weapons, civilian populations appear to be the main targets. The arguments are these: How do we destroy an "army" which exists only in the form of computers, missiles, and commanders? With a few concentrated warheads, how do we destroy isolated and separated factories? To which the arguments in opposition are these: The Russian people (for example) are not our enemies, so why must we destroy them to retaliate against their government—an enemy common to us both? Any war, no matter how sophisticated, will require physical conquest and probably hand to hand combat. The Soviets don't have two million men in the army for nothing. The problem abstractly is difficult. "It is not right to do evil that good may come." This proverb would appear to exclude the destruction of civilian populations in war, just as it excludes chemical and germ warfare. To the question, if the enemy plans or proceeds to destroy civilian populations, do we follow suit? *Tu Quoque* is a logical fallacy, and that indicates we should not.

If then we fight morally, and if fighting morally necessitates losing, is it the duty of virtue to lose a war where evil is needed to win?

856. We are free and we are afraid, because freedom involves choice and choice means the probability, at many points, of error and failure. And since our pride can be more easily reconciled to slavery than to failure, we call out to be enslaved—in a disguised way which will still allow us to assert that we are free.

857. The life of man contains success and failure. Art that presents only successes or failures exclusively is false art. True art must present ideals and possibilities and goals, and it must present the real methods by which those things can be obtained—trial and error, repeated attempts, perseverance—in short, how to endure success and failure. Art should teach reality: the most likely paths to success, the fact that not every journey down a given path succeeds. Art of the always-succeeding or always-failing character cannot teach human beings much.

858. The physical world and the human body are artificial places of temporary existence for the soul, and the soul adjusts to them and their limitations. The world is a passing artifice, a metaphor, like building blocks for the infant soul to learn about itself through what it constructs. So, even though truth and reality—the soul, God, the soul's savior—are non material, they are revealed to our understandings in material forms partly—human bodies, a pillar of fire, the wonders of creation, the incarnation. And since the soul was made to adjust to flesh and symbol, it can easily adjust to art and the artificial existences presented in fiction. In the same way, if we would open our eyes and ears, we would let the plants and animals of the world speak to us in praise of their maker. For man is not the only creature who exclaims, "I am fearfully and wonderfully made."

859. There is great truth in the oboes of Beethoven, but how can

you prove it?

860. The first thing we do when we meet people is to pigeon-hole them, usually into an unfavorable category — for we are hard hearted. "She's a klutz, he's cheap, she's stuck up, he's a big nothing, she's a gold digger, he's compulsive." Next, whenever we see our new acquaintances, we put on our pigeon-hole glasses ("Here comes the klutz, there's that cheapskate, I see Miss Stuckup"), and do our best to prevent seeing them for who they really already *are*, and we would never dream of encouraging them to live up to their potential of variety. This inflexible stereotyping seems to be much more characteristic of my generation than of past ones. What has made us into such blind and snotty wretches?

861. I read today about a man who wanted to live to be 200 years old. To accomplish this, he ate warfarin — an anticoagulant used in rat poison — and died at 33.

862. Then they begin to cry out and ask, "Who will save us from the works of our own hands?

863. Because of the hardness of hearts, sometimes screaming must precede weeping; and weeping, happiness.

864. The desire to eat your cake and have it too constitutes one of the basic elements of human nature. How we hate the fact that some choices preclude others. We want two (or three) irreconcilable things, so in frustration we become indecisive. Our fear of failure compounds our problems because it adds to our dislike of exclusionary choices and makes us uncomfortable with free will itself. Free will means choice; choice means inevitable mistakes along the way. But failure, loss and imperfection are necessary (and sometimes, if we knew all and could see clearly, desirable) parts of life, for they are the greatest teachers and improvers of the heart.

865. The difference between decoration and art is that decoration looks nice and pleases the eye, while art pleases and ennobles the soul. Decoration makes a room better; art makes a man better. Art speaks softly of truth—sometimes ineffable truth such as that of beauty or the magic of nature, while decoration sits silently, smiles, and looks pretty. A photograph can be art, when the subject, composition, and perspective combine to speak to the heart and soul and mind. But most photos—even the supposedly artsy ones—are just snapshots, or glorified snapshots.

866. What is the object of education at, say, the high school level? The college level? Graduate level? Is it a job skill, or functional literacy, or social homogeneity? Or should we speak of truth, humanity, culture, direction, wisdom, understanding, compassion? Most students out of high school lack the ability to think logically. Shouldn't that be a goal of education at that level?

867. When someone opposes you or disagrees with something you say, take a minute before you begin a battle to win him over, and ask yourself, what basis does he use for opposing me? We usually assume that a disagreement arises from a sincere and thought out intellectual difference. But many oppositions arise from envy, ignorance of issues or facts or words; a personal, programmed reaction to a word, term, or concept you have used; a dislike of yourself and hence of all your ideas; a partial knowledge which has led to a wrong conclusion; belief in something not true; or a prejudice which cannot be reconciled with your assertion. Only by understanding both the reason for and the substance of the opposition can you hope to overcome it.

868. You are blind men buying telescopes and bickering over magnification, resolution, contrast, and chromatic aberration. What you need are new eyes, not new lenses.

869. We have formed many of our opinions through prejudice

or hasty generalization or blind acceptance, but whenever our opinions are challenged, we demand exact, full, and incontrovertible proofs before we will allow even a doubt to enter our heads.

870. Law and popular opinion are the two great rulers of most people's lives, values, beliefs, and morals—and desires and satisfactions. Think of the activity around you—the fads, the dresses from designers, "I want what everyone else is buying, doing, wanting," "What is legal is moral," peer pressure. Our instinctively imitative learning methods are compounded by the psychological pressure to be normal and liked by others. Desire to be popular is but a sub facet of the desire to be happy. Advertisers teach that happiness comes through materialism because that moves products. When law or opinion fail to give guidance, personal, selfish, instantaneous feeling or urge is obeyed.

Solution—1) educate people to think ideally, beyond law and opinion and 2) teach them that highest goal is to serve God, to love him and other people. Other goals—wealth, power, goods, happiness—are wrong and deceitful motivators, 3) establish the highest and best law and opinion so that the weak slaves of them will live as well as possible until they can be taught to see beyond them. People will look to you, and say, "Your God will be my god," or they will see you groveling in the world for money or power, and say, "Your god will be my god."

871. Scarcely any word (other than "love") is so violently and sorely abused as the word "need," which when used, is almost always filling in as a substitute for other words like "want," "desire," "lust after idly," "have an irrational caprice for," or "crave uselessly."

872. Most people really believe abstract truths only after they have seen them demonstrated concretely, either directly or through some very pertinent analogous experiment. False or rigged experiments convince people that an error or lie is true,

and no amount of pure reason will change their minds. Once a man believes he saw something happen, he will refuse to be undeceived, except through clearer demonstration.

873. Any action whatsoever, if described as possible for human beings, will be viewed as a call for imitation by some people. Thus, the representation of evil serves as a descriptive lesson for some, and does not automatically repel all who hear or read or see it.

874. We imitate a man's vices more often than his virtues because we have felt a previous inclination toward the vices and gladly use his example to support our desires against reason.

875. Man is by nature wicked and heartless. To make him a doctor, politician, lawyer, executive, or policeman does not change his nature or exalt him above it. Human nature is conquered only by long personal struggle regardless of station. So why are you surprised, O naive one, when these people are crooked and unethical? Are you confusing money and power—the enemies of virtue—with virtue itself? Or do you consider it ironic that someone who knows the law and its punishments should ignore it or break it or manipulate it? How then do you react to your own behavior?

876. You must have feet if you want to have toes.

877. Whenever you formulate a moral precept, write it down to instruct the world; then ask yourself, "Why do I not practice or live up to this?" Our own lives furnish the nearest example of the failure of our own ideals.

878. We learn many lessons unwillingly, and once we learn them we gladly and quickly forget them until they are once again forced upon us against our will.

879. Resist the pressure and the temptation to measure yourself

by the world; avoid seeking the approval or the goals of the world. The things of the world are capricious and ephemeral, and most importantly, often wrong, if not evil.

880. How exciting and wonderful is a new friend, who will listen to all of your favorite anecdotes with interest and enthusiasm, because he has not yet heard them five hundred times.

881. The manufacturers which supply every hobby have a strong tendency to invent products or features that serve only marginal purposes. These gimmick products are unnecessary — but since all hobby equipment is by definition unnecessary, criticism becomes difficult and apparently arbitrary. Look at stereo equipment, camera accessories, fishing supplies — there's always some little item to buy to keep the flame going (both in your heart and in the industry's pocketbook).

882. Any emotion, feeling, or desire, in order to be sustained, must be periodically renewed or refreshed. Thus love requires repeated pledges and acts of affection and thoughtfulness — whether a husband brings roses or candy or the wife tries a new hairdo or main dish for hubbie's sake. Jobs, hobbies, and other interests are the same, and require something "new, different, and exciting" — just as the advertisers claim. They know about human nature.

883. A lot of misunderstanding about human motivation and behavior arises from the failure to recognize the real extent of the desire for superiority. The nose-in-the-air syndrome results in many surprising choices, rejections, and frustrations.

884. Re Pascal, Lafuma #759: Our tiniest sins, which we perhaps scarcely imagined harmful to ourselves or others, can continue to damage human hearts for many years, or even for generations. The law has an egg shell skull theory; life ought to recognize an egg shell heart theory — that we might henceforth realize how sensitive some are to the idle, careless blows we give them.

885. Few people employ their minds as reasoning organs. Most use them merely for warehouses of prejudices, idle tales, trivial information, false but attractive ideas, and as machines to change new ideas to agree with old ones. Sometimes you can watch another person struggle to fit some new information into his thought and belief patterns; he has already decided what answers he wants and is trying to manipulate you into giving them. When you say anything close to what he wants to hear, he reinforces it and files it away. All else is dropped into the ash can of forgottenhood and oblivion. The tendency to seek pattern and coherence from facts is not all wrong—there must be over-all consistency in truth. But we must seek openheartedly for the truth first—not seize upon some pleasant belief and then insist that all reality conform to it. "Do not pain us with the truth," cries the world; "give us something to believe which will deliver us from restraint and from responsibility for our acts and which will exalt our egos by proving us superior to others."

886. A word to the wise is sarcastic.

887. Even the finest wood cannot be nailed to dirt.

[January, 1981; age 30]

888. If you don't look back on your past life with a certain amount of regret, you haven't learned anything.

889. Only in the process of correcting mistakes do we really learn anything. (This is merely an alternate of "Success makes men proud; failure makes them wise.")

890. Pain always results when reality confronts imagination.

891. All make believe relationships must come to an end when the dreamer wakes, even when he has been dreaming with his eyes open.

892. The easy way up is seen only from the top of the mountain. — Proverb.

893. Only he who thinks he knows is truly ignorant. He who knows that he is ignorant and that he needs knowledge knows a valuable thing.

894. The first problem in communication is not to say clearly what you mean, but to mean something clear.

895. A piece of green or waterlogged wood will not burn by itself, but in the presence of good, seasoned wood, it will dry out and burn and give heat and light.

896. Sometimes the way a question is formulated prevents us from understanding the problem or from arriving at the right answer. To ask, What was the cause of that? can lead us on the search for a single cause in a situation where multiple causes exist. We must ask the right questions in order to arrive at truth.

897. Saying so is not making so.

898. Small spark; big fire.

899. All material things are merely dirt, refined and painted.

900. A bottomless bucket takes a long time to fill.

901. It was late at night when Darxul added these to *The Book of One Hundred Lies*:
    21. I was only kidding.
    22. I love you for yourself. Your good looks, power, and money have nothing to do with it.

902. Evil judges make all laws bad.

903. They believe that by extended deliberation they will make a

better choice; but deliberation, no matter how extensive, based upon erroneous principles, will never yield a better choice.

904. We don't understand the real nature of life because our minds are filled with cubby holes and life consists of a giant tapestry, textured and interwoven. We keep trying to label everything in absolute terms by a single word. Our thinking is becoming automatic, like the domino effect—plop, plop, plop. That's no way to truth or understanding.

905. People are starting to believe the advertisers and the world the advertisers present. Advertising stresses emotions and externals. People desire with all their hearts to believe that they can *buy* happiness, youth, beauty, and admiration.

906. Salvation isn't free; it's just prepaid.

907. Rock music is played to the body; it is designed to thump you into a state of euphoric narcosis, where nothing matters. Popular music is played to the heart, or at its best, to the mind; its intention is to touch common feelings (happiness, love, sorrow) and to affirm that some things in life do matter. Classical music is played to the soul; it proclaims an ordered universe where everything matters and in which a man can surpass himself and his feelings to see and to reach for the perfect. It is one of the very few means for exalting a person without making him proud.

908. He said we live in a world of sheep and asses. The sheep go along with whatever all the other sheep are going along with. There is no need to think or feel; but they take comfort in knowing that whatever they do, a hundred others are doing the same thing. Thus are guilt and ridicule diluted or prevented. The asses, on the other hand, rebel against anything the sheep are doing. When the sheep go, the asses stop, and no tugging or bleating will move them. When the sheep stop, the asses go.

909. Theory and practice seldom sleep in the same bed.

910. Whether intended or not, the result of recent technology has been to keep us ever increasingly from the labor of thinking. Thinking is hard work, so we use our technology to avoid it. I don't mean using calculators to avoid adding and subtracting, although that, too, is a symptom. Rather, we invent mind-occupying amusements—television, radio, motion pictures, automobiles, sports events. We never just sit around in the semi-dark and think. Modern information sources leave no time to think. A television news story or report is condensed from its complex reality into twenty seconds of oversimplification, and then before we can examine what has been dumped upon us, a new story is being presented.

911. The reason of the universe directs us toward God, because God made our minds and the universe.

912. The unsaved are walking tombs; we must call forth their souls to life.

913. Christ our gardener has uprooted us from the forest of vanities and transplanted us into the holy garden of God.

914. We describe rather than evaluate, measure rather than judge. Evaluation and judgment require the courage of moral commitment. The world wants only the safe facts, the comfortable knowledge.

915. Instead of building rails on the staircase, we pass out band aids to those who fall off. We are afraid of being called fanatics if we warn them of their danger, and after all, all, we say, everyone must find his own way. Everyone has a right to fall off.

916. A limb cannot be put back on the tree.

917. Think of the "social class" of the people with whom Christ gladly associated, and then get your nose out of the air.

918. The world has many delights; but more delightful still is God, the maker of the world's delights.

919. This is the age of aristocratic democracy, in which one purchases his social status by the label on his jeans.

920. Art should be a focusing lens, not simply a mirror of reality.

921. Art is a mirror of belief. It reflects the soul that creates it.

922. Conditioned consumption. We are trained to seek and buy and possess without regard to real need or use or satisfaction. A general psychological hunger is instilled into us, so we, out of habit and reflex, buy something every time we enter a store. We never believe the advertisers when they tell us their products will bring us happiness, but when we are unhappy, we buy often, and we buy a lot. But the desire is in the soul and cannot be satisfied by plastic and cardboard.

923. One of the most important truths we can learn is that while we can see only in a straight line, God can see around the corner.

924. We must be careful of our habits of thought, or we will always be thinking in the same channel. Every new event will automatically "prove" the truth of our pet theory without the need for examination, everything will become expected, typical, or ordinary. We will lose the sense of fine distinction, but more, the sense of awe and wonder at the complexity and variety of life. We will grow proud, disgusted and cynical, and bigoted and wrong.

925. Not only do we have a tendency to see other people as types, but we have a tendency to become types ourselves. The pressures of conformity and imitation and the ease of selecting a

life style already set out make us reject the difficulty of developing a personal being and character. The availability in mass of certain cultural items (books, music, art) also force certain choices upon us. Few people read William Law or Thomas a Kempis because their books are not in every store. Most people think, do, and buy what they see other people thinking, doing, and buying.

926. A kind heart is more than philosophy.

927. Gravity works every time.

928. The tendency in society now is to see one another as objects rather than as people. "Oh, I want a pretty one with fashionable clothes and blonde hair." "He goes so well with that car."

929. We make ourselves miserable by pursuing happiness.

930. Technology is the blessing and the illness of modern life.

931. Aristotle has said rightly that "all men desire knowledge," but it is also true that not all men desire truth. Many are happiest with false knowledge.

932. Many false religions can be detected by the fact that they are irrational. Truth, and religious truth is included, has a basic consistency and rationality to it. Christianity can be distinguished from superstition because Christian faith is grounded upon reasonable, sensible inferences and its doctrines are open to being inquired about. Some things in the faith are above reason and some cannot be understood fully, but none go against reason. Indeed, part of the Great Commandment is that we shall serve God with all of our understanding. Trust him thoughtfully.

933. The man shoveled madly to move the soil away from around him, only soon to discover himself in a pit.

934. Why do people ride roller coasters? Especially, why do they ride the violent, painful ones, which can only imaginatively be called fun? First, for the satisfaction of excitement addiction. The rush caused by being thrilled is similar to other chemical addictions in that a psychological desire for more and more is established, and in that increasing "doses" of the drug are required for continued satisfaction. This explains such phenomena as all-day riders, coaster addicts, and the search for ever more thrilling rides or experiences. Next, in addition to this goal of personal thrills, many young men use wild rides as instruments of romance. That a woman is likely to fall in love with a man with whom she shares a fearful, stressful experience has been well known for some time. Fear is an aphrodisiac for women. So if a youth takes a girl with him on a wild roller coaster, she is much more likely to fall in love with him than if he takes her to a miniature golf course. This, by the way, is also the reason for the popularity of horror movies. Lastly, riding roller coasters is a rite of passage for adolescents. The more vicious and extreme the ride, the better for this purpose. A young person declares his manhood by holding his arms in the air as the ride reaches its most punishing and "dangerous" point. He may not have fun per se, but the affirmation of masculinity is certainly to be described as enjoyable.

935. Writing a dissertation is like building a sand castle when you know the tide is coming in. It's as fun as having your wisdom teeth pulled; it speeds along like a snail crossing flypaper.

936. Every offer presents two dangers—first, that it will be rejected; and second, that it will be accepted. Although acceptance is usually seen as a positive, the hurt of rejection and the pain of performance can be of equal severity. The solution to this conundrum is to make a sincere offer (eliminating or reducing the pain of performance) and then to trust the decision to the will of God (reducing or eliminating the hurt of rejection).

937. When the water is up to your neck, your shoes are wet.
—Proverb

938. If you can understand a cat, you can understand a woman;
and if you can understand a woman, you can understand yourself.

939. "The two great disappointments in life are not getting what
you want, and getting it." This is one of the profoundest pieces
of philosophy I have come across in some time. What it teaches
us, though, is not that life is futile and destined for frustration,
but that personal desire—the will of the self—is not perceptive
enough to know what is the best thing or path to choose. Instead of seeking what we want, we should seek what God
wants us to have, for only he knows what is best for us.

940. The truth shows different appearances from different angles. —Proverb

[January 1, 1982; age 31]

941. His eye was attracted to a bright yellow towel; so he bought
it. But it was thin and rough compared to his old brown towel.
When he chose a wife, therefore, he paid no attention to her
looks.

942. A man tests gold to see if it is pure; gold tests a man to see
if he is pure.

943. Let your heart be filled with the Word of God, and you
won't need to have your ears filled with the words of men. Beware of flattery in every disguise.

944. Why did men choose to explore space instead of the
oceans? Partly because of the glamour, of course. But more, because the space program was religiously motivated. It was pursued in hopes of finding firm support for evolution, which is

the religion of many scientists.

945. The soil of pity often nurtures a flower of contempt, but the soil of sympathy brings forth a flower of love.

946. Men too often marry a body instead of the girl who lives inside, and women too often marry a job instead of the man who holds it. Both fall in love with illusions — or better, with delusions.

947. "Don't I have the right to control my own property?" asked the man, beating his slave into unconsciousness.

948. The contest is often delivered to the man with the ready answer rather than to the man who is right.

949. People fit their actions to the names they are called.

950. Not the event, but the attitude.

951. Painted dirt, cardboard and plastic, mud and sand. For our brief time on earth shall we fondle and treasure these toys as if they were something of value?

952. What does a woman want in a man? One who is strong, confident, decisive, energetic, and a little unkind. Good looks and money help, too.

953. They are practicing to do well what is not worth doing even badly. (Technique over substance; how over what.)

954. They make a big pile of trash out of many little piles of trash and then say proudly, "See what we have done?"

955. After death, all men's hands are open; but then it is too late for them to give.

956. Men laugh at a dung beetle pushing his possession along, but they take their own possessions seriously. And are they any less burdened by them?

957. Man is distinguished by his love of externals.

958. The person who says, "What you're doing is good," is as helpful as the person who uses the hammer and nail.

959. We are always surprised when we must suffer, when instead we should be surprised when we can feel joy.

960. Life is amusing, but amusing is such a sad way that it would be cruel to laugh.

961. They study carefully all the volumes on how to choose a spouse wisely, and after the last volume has been thoroughly read and marked, they put it down and choose someone with good looks.

962. Much modern art (in the wide sense) provides the reassurance of despair for those in love with despair.

963. Advertising does not merely exalt the self, it apotheosizes it.

964. Five years is the outside design limit on modern man. Cars, furniture, air conditioners, marriages, clothing styles, movie stars, fads—all are designed to pass away in five years or less. Such is the tragedy of unexamined novelty—change for its own sake, the worship of the new.

965. Advertising creates an obsession for the unobtainable as people engage in an intense struggle to find or become one of those perfect people whom advertising continuously declares to exist. Those people are always bright, beautiful, happy, refreshed; they are never sweaty, pimply, vomiting, or de-

pressed—never even tired or sick for more than fifteen seconds (only until the product can work).

966. Hope is the great torturer of human souls, yet it is also the delight of life.

967. When the fire of love goes out in your marriage, often it's because you've stopped hauling in the wood.

968. Life: a befuddled rehash of old clichés.

969. Discrimination is the great principle of clear thinking.

970. It is in the struggle between duty and pleasure that you find out who you are.

971. Falsehood and evil are quickly gaining ground not simply because people love them naturally, but because those ideas are so frequently and well articulated that they become attractive.

972. Experiment has taken the place of wisdom and judgment, though experiment is useless without them. Evaluation and abstract values have been replaced by pragmatic, empirical success as a good by definition. Statistics replace reason. Opinion polls are the new standards of truth and morality. Those who manipulate polls and statistics are smiling.

973. Familiarity with something—an acquaintance with or awareness of something over time—leads us to a belief in the thing or in the truth of an idea. Such repeated affirmation is the basis of brainwashing—though the process is much more subtle and drawn out in ordinary life.

  We tend also to support the protagonist in a book or film because we are so well acquainted with him. Focus creates a sympathetic presentation. Evil, by becoming familiar, comes to be at first tolerated, and then approved. "Whatever is, is right" is a profound (though horrible) tendency in human psychology.

974. Real meaning first gave way to the impression of meaning. Vague or ambiguous statements that seemed to mean something, but didn't, took over on account of their frequent use, their ease, their attractiveness, their ease of being used for one's devious ends. Now even the impression or appearance of meaning has given way to irrelevance of meaning. Advertisers, politicians, interest groups, ordinary people often use expressions or make statements consisting almost entirely of emotive formulations which convey little or no meaning. We are becoming conditioned to this, and expect it. Specific meaning is now viewed as unnecessary or even non-existent. Man soon will have a vocabulary of 500,000 synonyms for *grunt* and *growl*. We are letting words do our non-thinking for us. And note that we have replaced "I think" with "I feel."

975. Advertisers teach us to be dissatisfied and to have problems because they can then present their products as solutions.

976. Why do we continually fool ourselves into thinking that if we can describe something or pronounce its name, we therefore understand it?

977. Theater art provides a structured method of disengaging the structures of real life (that is, an artificial structure is substituted for the real one), in order to act out or examine other roles and attitudes which might be dangerous or frightening to try in one's life. It is a psychodrama giving freedom from social rules because "it's only in fun" and it allows the expression of hidden beliefs or the trying of opposite feelings.

978. Why do you pine when truth is opposed or ridiculed? Do you not know that truth must be opposed to make it more prominent and obvious, to purify it, to make you more loyal to it and more loving of it? The sword must be thrust into the sand to clean off the rust — and then how it shines!

979. It is not only the shouting arms from the rooftop but the bended knees in the inner room that praise him.

980. We must never forget that our perceptions are altered by our expectations and prejudices. A variety or example of this is the so-called self-fulfilling prophecy. "This will be fun," we say, or "This will be boring." And so, often, it is. Another variety is the demand we place on the external world to be consistent with what we know or think we know. "He is careless," we think, and then we proceed to interpret his every action in harmony with—nay, as a proof of—that conclusion.

981. Many people are almost child-like in their suggestibility. Tell them they're having fun and they'll believe it. Tell them you're wonderful and they'll believe it. Why? It is easier than inquiring and thinking. See *Rambler* 135.

982. A man rejoicing in the dim light of his own campfire cares not for the greater and purer light of the stars.

983. Some emotional pain is necessary or at least unavoidable by the fully human, because it is the price of humanity and wholeness; for pain is the natural reaction to the loss of value, and everyone ought to value things. Pain also is a great teacher—we pay attention and think and learn when we hurt, much more than when we laugh. And pain is often a prelude to building. Pain tears down the old shack of the feelings that they may be housed in a better place.

984. Strong or weak, beautiful or plain, distinguished or ordinary, intelligent or not, we are all creatures of his right hand, made in his image and with his love—made with a plan and for some purpose.

985. You are right to point out the mushroom growing among the grass, for it is beautiful and wonderful. But do not neglect the grass, nor fail to caress it also, just because it is common; it

too is lovely and notable, even if not rare. In a world of mush-rooms, a blade of grass would be remarked upon with interest and attention. View it, then — and all common things — in that way.

986. The worshipers of dogmatic uncertainty please themselves with believing nothing because they say they're free from the pressures and demands of consistency and moral restraint. People who believe in nothing are often executed but never martyred.

987. We become what we perceive.

988. There can be no wine unless a grape is broken.

989. Only in the ecstasies of self-congratulation is our true igno-rance revealed.

990. That a thinking being can be proud shows how ineffective thinking really is.

991. Marriage is a stack of lumber and a keg of nails: you have to build it yourself. If the roof leaks, look to the carpenters.

992. Etymologies are the semantic underwear of words.

993. Pain is the chalk, laughter the eraser.

994. Women are not morally worse than men — more calculating or more heartless — but they seem so because we expect them to be better.

995. The quiet, subtle, and thoughtful aspects of life are dying — or are being murdered — on account of the exaltation of the loud, the amplified, the exaggerated. Look at rock music, adver-tising, the plot and action of television and motion pictures, high fashion, or even common conversation. Where is anything

but hyperbole? A constant diet of extremes desensitizes us to fineness and detail. How attentively do we listen to rock music? How complex and interesting intellectually is television programming? No one pays attention to naked Truth anymore, standing there quietly in the corner, because she doesn't scream and spit and stomp her feet.

996. The visual media present us with pre-packaged imagination, in one sense usurping our intellectual prerogatives and stilling our power to think. All we can do is either choose or imitate; we can no longer create for ourselves.

997. Help me, O Lord, to trust not only in your will, but in your timetable.

998. Do not *tell* me what you believe; *show* me.

999. If you pour for yourselves, you'll have full glasses; if you pour for each other, you'll have full hearts.

1000. Head in the clouds, feet on the ground: wise man. Feet in the air, head in the dirt: fool.

1001. Take your wife as from the hands of God and treat her as befits such a gift.

⌘⌘⌘

About the Author

Robert Harris was born in Los Angeles, California in 1950. He began to write these Glimmerings at age 23, when he was in graduate school completing a master's degree. He continued writing down his observations during a period of scant employment (address label typist in a seed company, real estate salesman, very part-time professor), and then back into graduate school, where at great length he obtained a PhD in English.

Fifteen years as a college and university professor and seven years as an instructional designer gave him additional thoughts for recording — which you will find in *Glimmerings II*.

Now, Dr. Harris is "retired" (also known as writing and researching full time but without definite compensation). He lives in Tustin, California with his wife, Marie.

Colophon

Body text set in Book Antiqua 11 point
Headings set in **Arial Black**

Book Antiqua is Microsoft's version of
Palatino, a classic font
of which the author is excessively fond.

A semiotic interpretation of Book Antiqua / Palatino
is that it exhibits a formal, serious ethos
which transfers to the content,
enhancing and underscoring
whatever intellectual quality
exists in the content itself.

In practical terms,
this font is just very readable.

www.ingramcontent.com/pod-product-compliance
Lightning Source LLC
Chambersburg PA
CBHW060922040426
42445CB00011B/754